Play Bridge?

B ridge is principally a game of deduction. You do not need an exceptional memory or advanced mathematics. Some cards are visible, some not. As the unseen cards are progressively revealed, you use specified clues to draw precise conclusions or informed judgements about the cards that you still cannot see.

Bridge is a partnership game. The basic contest is between two sides of two people each. Bridge players need the social skills to bring out the best in a partner, and have to visualise the problems faced both by partner and opponent. That may explain why many people who are successful in business also enjoy bridge.

Bridge and chess are the world's leading mind sports. If you are tempted to scoff at the idea that bridge is a sport, accept for a moment that the brain is merely one part of the body. Playing will improve your mental fitness, and the fitter your brain the easier you will find it to play. You can choose whether you want to play bridge as a social pastime or as a competitive sport where you strive to succeed. Either way, in common with the best of the physical sports, you will find bridge has excitement, thrills and spills, an attractive mix of luck and skill, photo-finishes, rules and discipline, a range of tournaments from local club to world champion-ships, long-lasting friendships and the comradeship of memorable teams.

Bridge and its Laws are the same across the world. You can go on holiday or move home and instantly make new friends through the game. On the internet you can play bridge any time of the day or night, and the four players at the 'table' can actually be sitting in four different continents of the world. You can play without leaving your home – a particular attraction for the house-bound or the disabled, or where time is short – and English is the international language of bridge.

Bridge, once learned, lasts a lifetime. You can enjoy bridge as a youngster to your eighties and beyond. For the Home Internationals England has fielded a teenager and a player over the age of seventy in the same team. As each new deal represents a new challenge, bridge players never get bored by the game.

Bridge is cheap to play. You need only a pack of cards, perhaps a pencil and paper to keep score, and three other bridge players. I have played bridge on a mountain-top, in the Ferris Wheel of Vienna, on the internet, on trains and planes, on buses and boats, against billionaires (Bill Gates of Microsoft was one) and paupers, in prison (as a visitor!) and in the House of Commons.

Take the trouble to learn and you will not regret it.

Patrick Jourdain, Cardiff 2005

Contents

1
Getting Started

New terms are in italics and defined in the glossary.
The number of men and women playing bridge is similar, but throughout this book
the masculine pronoun will be used in order to avoid the clumsy 'he or she.'

Bridge is a card game for four people sitting round a table, where the players facing each other are partners. We refer to the four people and their position at the table by the points of the compass: West, North, East and South.

North and South are *partners,* on the same side, playing against East and West, their *opponents.* A plus score for one side is an equal minus for their opponents. What is good for North is good for South, but bad for East and West. The *deal* of a pack of 52 cards will give each player 13 cards, called their *hand.*

There are two types of bridge, very similar, and this book covers both. *Rubber bridge* is played when there is only one table in play. It can be, but does not have to be, played for money. As with poker the luck of the deal (where one side receives better cards than the other) can outweigh the skill factor in the short term, but skill will determine the winners in the long run. *Duplicate* bridge can be played when there is more than one table in play. Here the luck of the deal is eliminated by reproducing identical deals at different tables and then comparing the score of one side at one table with the score achieved at another table by a side holding identical cards. The deal is normally replicated by putting each player's hand for one deal into a separate slot in a *board* (see the illustration at the top of page 6). The board is passed from table to table where different groups of four players receive the same deal without further dealing. When playing duplicate players must retain their own cards during play so they can return them to the board exactly as received, ready to pass the deal to another table.

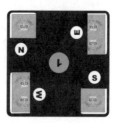

Duplicate gives much more emphasis to the skill element of bridge. In bridge clubs, duplicate bridge is more common than rubber. The winners are not known until the end of the session when the players will have moved to meet several different opposing pairs, and all will have played the same set of deals. The prizes are pre-determined. At duplicate bridge it is normal to choose your own partner, at rubber bridge it is common, though not compulsory, to *cut* (i.e. draw) for partners, using the same pack of cards with which you are intending to play, a procedure we now describe.

For bridge the pack of cards has no jokers, just the basic 52 cards. There are four suits: spades (♠), hearts (♡), diamonds (◇), and clubs (♣). Within each suit there are thirteen cards. In bridge, the ace always counts high, so the seniority within each suit, starting with the highest is:

To cut for partners each player selects a card, and when all have chosen, faces it. Taking the rank (ace down to 2) of the card as the main determining factor, the two highest will be partners, the next two will be their opponents, and any others wait for a game. If two cards have the same rank, then seniority of the suits is used to distinguish them. This ranking of the suits also arises in a phase of bridge that precedes the play of the cards, called the *bidding*. The order is alphabetical, starting with the junior suit, clubs, i.e. clubs, diamonds, hearts and then spades, the senior suit. This ranking is not relevant during the play of the cards at bridge.

In the diagram below five players wanting to play rubber bridge have cut the ace of clubs, the jack of diamonds, the jack of hearts, the three of spades and the seven of spades. The player who drew the lowly three will sit out. The player who drew the ace, as highest card, will have both a privilege and a responsibility, but who will partner the ace? As hearts are senior to diamonds, the player who cut the jack of hearts becomes the ace's partner.

The one who drew the highest card has a privilege and a responsibility. The privilege is choice of seat! The most comfortable, the one nearest the radiator or closest to the bar, make your choice. Partner must sit opposite, and the other two fill in the empty spots as they please. If you do not know the names of all the other players, introduce yourself.

The responsibility of the player who cut the highest card is to conduct the first deal. More than a century ago at whist, a precursor of bridge, a ritual was designed to avoid players fixing the deal. The procedure for shuffling the deck, cutting it, and dealing it is described in Appendix A. At duplicate the board indicates on it who is the dealer but the players often let whosoever wants the chore to do it at the beginning of the session (there is no further dealing once all boards are dealt). In some tournaments a computer predetermines the deals and the organisers arrange for the boards to be prepared in advance so the players don't have to do any dealing themselves.

When the deal has successfully been completed, or, at duplicate when a new board arrives, each player takes up their hand, and inspects it, without letting any other player see their cards. It is then normal, and makes life much easier later, to sort your 13 cards into suits, and within each suit into ascending order of cards with the highest to the left and behind. If you also put the four suits in ascending order there are two snags. Firstly the two red suits, hearts and diamonds, would be adjacent, and it is easy to make a mistake during play by failing to distinguish them. Secondly, another player with poor ethics might deduce something about your hand by seeing the position from where you later removed a card. Therefore we strongly advise putting the suits in any order that alternates black and red suits. A sorted bridge hand will look to the owner something like this:

The play of each deal of bridge actually has two phases. During the bidding players see only their own 13 cards. Then comes the play of the cards where one player's hand is visible for the other three to see (the *dummy*) and the unseen cards are revealed one at a time as *tricks* containing one card from each player. The bidding results with one partnership *(the declaring side)* having an undertaking (the *contract*) as to how many tricks it will make during the play. One player on the declaring side *(declarer),* with dummy faced opposite declarer, has to fulfil this contract by choosing the cards to play both from their own hand, and from dummy. Hence the name 'dummy' as the owner of the dummy hand simply follows the instructions of his partner, declarer, as to which card to play. The two players on the opposing side, whose objective is to prevent declarer fulfilling the contract, are called the *defenders.* The defender to declarer's left always plays the first card (the *lead*). Then dummy is revealed and the play proceeds. As bidding cannot be understood without knowing what happens during play, we start by describing the play of one deal.

Let us suppose the bidding concludes with South as declarer, and therefore North as dummy, and West on lead. West selects any card from his hand, and places it face upwards on the table for all to see. Playing rubber bridge it would be normal to play all cards into the centre of the table, but in duplicate, at the end of the play you must return your cards to the board exactly as they started, so players must keep their own cards by them.

After the lead has been made (by West, on this occasion) the player to the leader's left, in this case North, places their complete hand face upwards on the table as the dummy. The suits are placed in four separate columns, usually with the highest card closest to the owner of the hand and at the back, as illustrated below:

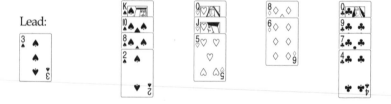

A trick consists of four cards, one contributed by each player, in order round to the left from the player who led to the trick. The suit of the card led determines the suit of this trick. In the illustration above, as West led the three of spades the first trick will be a spade trick. That means the other three players must each play a spade if they have one, the phrase is they must *follow suit.* In the example above, dummy is second to play, but declarer chooses which card dummy plays. Declarer must instruct dummy to play one of dummy's spades. If declarer calls for the king, this card must be played from dummy.

A player who has no card in the suit led may play any card in their hand, called a *discard.* The trick is won by the highest card played to the trick of the suit led to the trick. When all four cards have been played to the trick and the winner determined, the cards are turned face downwards.

Remember bridge is a partnership game. The object during the play is for your side to win as many tricks as possible. If you are last to play to a trick and your partner's card is already winning the trick it will usually be right to retain a higher card to use later in the play.

In duplicate bridge players must keep their own cards in front of them, and point the card turned face down in the direction of the side that won the trick (see next diagram). In rubber bridge where the cards were thrown in the middle of the table, the winner of the trick gathers them together to make one pile of four cards kept by him or by partner.

The player who won the trick leads to the next trick any card from their hand. You can now keep going until all the tricks have been played. As each player held 13 cards, and contributed one card to each trick, the total number of tricks is always 13. In the illustrations below one side has won 7 tricks, and the other has won 6.

At duplicate bridge the cards in front of a player at the end of play will look something like this:

In rubber bridge stacked tricks look like this:

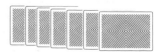

In the illustration of duplicate, the card played to the first trick is the one on the left. You can tell the opponents won this trick as the card runs from left to right. But this player's side won the second trick, and, as shown, seven in total. You check the number of tricks won by declarer to see if the contract was made. If so, declarer's side will receive a plus score for making the contract with the defenders losing the same number of points. If the contract failed, the scoring penalty for failure will be a plus score for the defending side with the declaring side losing these points.

After the score has been agreed, in rubber bridge all 52 cards are gathered together to be shuffled for a later deal. In duplicate each hand of 13 cards must be returned to the correct slot in the board, and the board passed to another table.

When the players receive a new board, they bid it seeing only their own 13 cards, and when the bidding is complete, play as before. But this time we introduce the concept of a *trump* suit.

The contract not only specifies the number of tricks declarer must make (the *level* of the contract), but can also specify one suit to have temporary priority over the other three suits during the play of this deal. This suit is the trump suit, and the trump suit is called the *denomination* of the contract. There are actually FIVE possible denominations because you can have any of the four suits as trumps, or you can have NO TRUMPS (as we did on the previous deal), i.e. no suit has precedence over the others.

The difference when the contract has named a trump suit is this: a trick is still won by the highest card played to the trick, UNLESS a trump is played to the trick, in which case the highest trump played to the trick wins the trick.

The rule that each player must follow suit still applies. So you can play a trump either when it is your lead, or compulsorily when someone else has led a trump, or when you have no card of the suit led to the trick. In this latter case, where the suit led was not a trump and you have no cards of the suit led as before you may play any card in your hand. But if you play a trump, even a tiny one, it will beat any card that is not a trump. If two or three players were out of cards of the suit led to the trick, and chose to play a trump, the higher trump played would win the trick.

It is good news for your side to have more trumps than the other side, indeed the more the merrier. The more trumps you have the quicker you find yourself out of cards in the other suits, and able to beat the opponents' high card with your trumps, however lowly. Try a couple of deals playing one with clubs as trumps, and another with diamonds as trumps, to understand this point. When dummy is faced it is a Law of Bridge that trumps must be placed on dummy's right, i.e. on the left as looked at by declarer. This is to help the other players remember what suit is trumps.

Having learned the mechanics of winning tricks with a trump suit or without, you are now ready to have a contract.

The bidding determines the contract and we have so far done no bidding. Fortunately for beginners there is a simplified version of bridge, designed for introducing schoolchildren to bridge, called *MiniBridge* where the play is identical to full bridge but there is no bidding. A simple arithmetic rule is used to decide who is declarer and the level of the contract, and declarer is allowed to see dummy BEFORE play starts, in order to choose trumps. Once the contract is determined play proceeds exactly as in full bridge.

The same arithmetic rule used in *MiniBridge* to determine declarer is also a method of estimating the trick-taking potential of a bridge hand used as a guide by players bidding in full bridge. It is called *'counting your points.'* This is nothing to do with scoring. It merely provides a rough guide to how many tricks you may expect to win when it comes to the play.

Most tricks are won by one of the four highest cards in any suit, namely the ace, king, queen or jack. Clearly a hand with plenty of these high cards will be more likely to win extra tricks during the play. When bridge first started teachers each had their own pet method of assessing how many tricks would be won. Fortunately for today's bridge players one method has swept all others aside. It is this: assign to each ace you hold in your hand a value of 4 points, to each king a value of 3 points, to each queen a value of 2 points, and for each jack a value of 1 point.

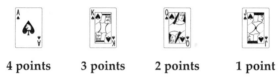

| 4 points | 3 points | 2 points | 1 point |

The total is that hand's *high-card point count*.
For example, suppose your hand of 13 cards was:

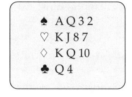

♠ A Q 3 2
♡ K J 8 7
◊ K Q 10
♣ Q 4

We digress for a moment on a matter of presentation. Ask a bridge-playing friend to write down a bridge hand. If they learned bridge only by playing and not by reading they may write the cards of one suit in a vertical column, as you would physically see them in dummy. But in newspapers and books the cards of one suit in a bridge hand are printed horizontally, with the suit symbol first and then the cards held in that suit starting with the highest, to the right of the symbol. The senior suit, spades, is given first, then hearts, diamonds and clubs, the junior suit.

So, in the diagram of a hand above, we mean the hand contains:

in spades the ace, queen, three and two;
in hearts the king, jack, eight and seven;
in diamonds the king, queen, and ten; and
in clubs the queen and four.

The high-card point count (*HCP* for short) of this hand is 17 (one ace worth 4 points, two kings worth 3 points each, three queens worth 2 points each, and one jack worth 1 point).

In MiniBridge the four players, starting with the dealer, and going round to the left, state how many points each holds. Have you worked

---

out what the total for the four players must be? It should always be 40 (the pack of cards has four suits, each with one ace, one king, one queen and one jack). If the total does not come to 40 one or more players has made an error counting their points, and all re-check. When the total comes to 40, the partnership with the most points is deemed the declaring side. If by sheer chance each side has exactly 20 points, then the deal is deemed a washout and there is a re-deal.

Usually, however, one side will have more than 20 points and that side is the declaring side. The player of that side who has the most points is designated declarer. If the players in the partnership have an equal number of points it is the one who first declared his points who is the declarer.

Once declarer is determined in MiniBridge the player opposite faces their hand as dummy. Declarer now chooses the denomination of the contract. Remember when choosing trumps quantity is much more important than quality in selecting the trump suit ('Never mind the quality, feel the width!') but this is for the TWO hands. You need to find out in which suit your side has the most cards, and then select that. A useful guide is that any suit with EIGHT cards between the two hands provides a satisfactory trump *fit*, whereas if the most number of cards you have in any one suit is seven then you should choose to have 'No Trumps'.

This key principle is illustrated below with two bridge hands opposite each other where the rank of the cards is concealed and only the *shape* (i.e. the number of cards in each suit) is shown.

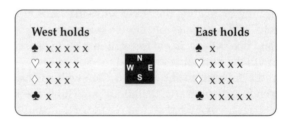

In this example West's longest suit is spades where he has five cards. East's longest suit is clubs, where he also has five cards. But the partnership's longest suit is hearts where they have a total of eight cards. It is therefore hearts that the partnership should choose as trumps. Once trumps are chosen it is a rule that dummy places that suit to his right, i.e. declarer's left, so players can easily remember what is trumps. In MiniBridge declarer is able to see both hands before making his choice, but when you come to full bridge bidding you have to locate the suit with most cards without seeing your partner's hand and that is much more difficult!

Here is another example, where West has the same shape as before but East's shape has been slightly changed, swapping the red suits:

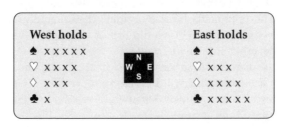

West holds
♠ x x x x x
♡ x x x x
♢ x x x
♣ x

East holds
♠ x
♡ x x x
♢ x x x x
♣ x x x x x

Again West's longest suit is spades, and East's longest suit is clubs, but now the partnership has no suit with as many as eight cards together, and in MiniBridge declarer should choose to have *no-trumps* as the denomination of the contract.

Note that you cannot see the layout of the cards held by the opponents. If your side had only seven trumps, the opponents would have the remaining six trumps, and there is a risk that one opponent might have most of these six, putting you at a disadvantage in the play. When, however, your side has eight trumps, the opponents have only five, and that gives your side sufficient advantage in the play to make it worthwhile selecting the suit as trumps.

What about the level of the contract? There are differing versions of MiniBridge. In some declarer chooses the level of the contract, and the key thing you need to know here is that the scoring rewards more ambitious contracts, *provided* the contract is made. For example, the highest reward would go to a contract to make *all* 13 tricks, known as the *grand slam*. But clearly the opponents only need to win one trick to defeat the grand slam, and then declarer's side loses points instead of winning them.

It is a Law of Bridge that all contracts must be to make more than half the tricks, i.e. at least 7 of the 13. We actually say how many tricks more than six. So the level of contract can be anywhere between 1 (i.e. an undertaking to make at least seven tricks) up to 7 (an undertaking to take all 13, the grand slam). In MiniBridge declarer may choose the highest level that the player is confident of fulfilling.

Most beginners find making this choice too difficult initially, but you can use the number of points the partnership holds to make a good guess at how many tricks will be made. The crucial relationship between points and tricks is this: *3 points will on average win one extra trick.*

So, if you take the point count of the partnership and divide by three you will have a sensible target for the level of the contract (round up to the nearest whole number, to teach declarers to be bold!)

How do we arrive at this key relationship between points and tricks?

First suppose your side had all the aces, all the kings, all the queens and three of the jacks, i.e. 39 points. You would certainly expect to take all 13 tricks. Now suppose your side has one point above the average of 20, i.e. 21 points. The opponents have marginally less, namely, 19 points. So when it comes to the play you would expect your side to win 7 of the 13 tricks and the other side to win only six.

Of course, this is only a very approximate guide, and as you learn more about the game you will become more skillful at assessing how many tricks your side can take. Meanwhile, rely on this guide, and you will be surprised how accurate it is.

After one intensive lesson you can play MiniBridge. Try it out.

Summary of MiniBridge

- Cut for partners. The highest card cut deals first. Left of dealer shuffles, right of dealer cuts the deck towards dealer who deals one card at a time face downwards, starting with the opponent on his left. When the deal is complete check you have 13 cards, then, keeping them hidden from the other players, sort your hand into suits (keeping suits of the same colour apart) and into ascending order of the rank of card within each suit. As you do so, count your high-card points (ace = 4, king = 3, queen = 2, jack = 1).

- In MiniBridge, starting with the dealer and going round to the left, each player states their point count. The total must come to 40. The side with the most points is the declaring side, the player of that side with most points is declarer. Declarer's partner places his hand face upwards on the table in columns of suits for everyone to see. Declarer chooses as trumps the suit with most cards between the two hands together. If there is no suit with at least eight cards together, declarer should choose to have no trumps. If declarer has chosen a trump suit dummy moves that suit to be on his right, i.e. declarer's left as he looks at dummy.

- The level of contract is the number of points the partnership holds divided by three and rounded up to the nearest whole number. That defines the minimum number of tricks declarer must make in the play. The opponents' (defenders') objective is to prevent declarer fulfilling the contract.

- Once the contract has been determined the player to declarer's left leads to the first trick. Dummy plays cards as instructed by declarer. The player who wins a trick leads to the next trick.

- At the end of play check how many tricks declarer has made. If this equals or exceeds the contract, the declaring side wins points (we tackle scoring later). If the contract fails, the declaring side loses points to the opponents.

Exercise on Getting Started

In all the exercises in this book, the answers are given immediately after the questions. You might like to cover the exercise pages with a piece of paper and slide it down so you don't peep at the answers too soon!

Q1 How many high-card points does this bridge hand have?

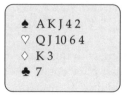

♠ A K J 4 2
♡ Q J 10 6 4
♢ K 3
♣ 7

A1 14 points (one ace = 4, two kings = 6, one queen = 2, two jacks = 2, total 14).

Q2 What is wrong with this bridge hand?

♠ K Q 6 3
♡ J 10 7 6
♢ 9 4
♣ A 7 4 2

A2 The hand has 14 cards. Impossible!

Q3 If your partnership has 35 high-card points, how many tricks would you expect it to take in the play?

A3 12 tricks (a contract to make at least 12 tricks is called a *small slam*).

Q4 If this is the shape of two bridge hands, declarer and dummy, what should declarer choose as trumps?

A4 Choose diamonds as trumps.

Q5 With these two hands what should you choose as trumps, and what should the level of contract be?

A5 The contract should be 9 tricks (26 points divided by 3 and rounded up) with no trumps (there is no suit with eight cards between the two hands). As declarer actually says how many tricks in excess of six are to be made this contract would be described as 'Three No-trumps' or 3NT.

Q6 When can the player with the dummy hand choose what card to play from his own hand?

A6 Never! Dummy must only play his cards as instructed by declarer.

Q7 How many different contracts are there at bridge?

A7 35. There are seven different levels and five different denominations. All combinations are possible so there are 7 x 5 = 35 possible different contracts. Every contract at bridge must be one of these 35.

2

The Basics of Card Play

We have done no bidding yet, but you know that the bidding concludes with a contract, an undertaking to make at least a specified number of tricks, with a known trump suit. Declarer has to fulfil the contract for the partnership seeing both his own cards and the dummy hand, and choosing the cards to play from both.

This allows declarer to plan how the contract might be made. Declarer cannot see the layout of the opponents' cards, nor does declarer know how the opponents will play. This will be revealed trick by trick. Either of these factors may determine whether the contract succeeds or fails. But it is quite possible for the contract to be secure, whatever the layout of the unseen cards, and however the opponents play, provided declarer plays his cards to best effect.

The key element to a plan is estimating how many tricks you can make for sure, and then seeking the best chance of increasing this number to achieve the contract. To start on this task look at one suit only and assess the number of tricks you can make in that one suit. Look at the various diagrams below and see whether you can work out how many tricks you expect to make with each holding. First, a really simple one, to establish the principles:

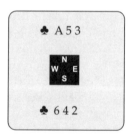

Suppose the contract is no-trumps, that you are declarer as South, so the cards in the North hand opposite are in dummy and visible for all to see. You cannot see the cards of East or West, but know that they have the remaining cards in this suit. How many club tricks do you expect to take?

Answer: One and only one (the ace will win a trick for sure, but the other cards must be beaten by the opponents' cards).

Is there any circumstance in which you could win more than one trick? Think about the cards you cannot see. We have six clubs, one sure winner and the rest very small. The opponents have the remaining seven clubs. Their cards beat any of yours except the ace. The only way you can make more than one club trick is if the opponents, towards the end of the play, throw away (discard) so many clubs that after you play a club and put the ace on, perhaps the other side have no clubs left. Then your lowly clubs are winners. This would be a grievous error by the opponents. In general, as you see various layouts, assume the opponents play to their own best interests. First learn plays that may succeed irrespective of what the other side does, rather than hoping for some error from them. Rely on errors from the other side when it is your only hope!

This next diagram may look as easy but it actually brings up a highly important technique of play, called the *finesse*. How many tricks do you expect with this holding:

You still have one big card, the king, but the opponents now have one card to beat it, the ace. How can you win the king without it getting clobbered by the opponent's ace? You don't know where the ace is, only that West or East must have it.

First thought, lead the king and hope the opponent with the ace does not play it on your king. Bad idea! The opponent with the ace will almost certainly choose to play it on your king. Second idea, lead a small card from the South hand, and hope the opponent with the ace plays it. Poor idea! An opponent might have the ace as his only card and be forced to play it, but that is extremely unlikely. The great majority of the time he will have a choice and know that playing a lower card will win the trick as he can see that dummy has only small cards to play.

Third idea, lead a small card from the North hand opposite the king and plan to play the king if East, the opponent who plays second to the trick, does not play the ace. Very good idea! The fundamental difference is that this plan forces East to make his choice of card to play before you as South choose whether to play your king. If East has the ace this means he cannot capture your king. East may choose to win the trick with the ace, in which case you retain the king for later. East, having won the trick, will have the choice of what to lead to the next trick but provided you can later win some trick you can then choose to play a further club and make your king, now the highest card in the suit.

But what, you are surely asking, if West holds the missing ace? Then when you play the king from the South hand he will beat it with his ace, and you will make no tricks in the suit.

Now comes the crucial point. When you lead the suit West will always be playing after South and, in effect the king is dead whenever West has the ace. (There is an exception if West was left with the ace as the only card in the suit. In that case, very unlikely here, as it gives East five or six cards in the suit, the winning play is to play a low card from the South hand.)

So you now have a plan of how to make the king when East has the missing ace, a plan that fails when West has the ace, but in that latter case there is no alternative decent plan. Given that it is equally likely that the ace is with East or West, your play, when executed on many different deals, can be expected to succeed half the time. Half the time you make one trick, on the other occasions you make no trick. The trick-taking potential of the holding is said to be 'half a trick'!

Now try this holding:

Clearly there are two tricks available because you ensure the ace and king are played to different tricks, but the opponents will have the cards to win any other trick.

That gives what seems some odd arithmetic. The ace on its own is worth one trick, the king on its own is worth half a trick, but with both ace and king you have two tricks. That is why an ace is worth four points, more than one trick (remember, three points = one trick). Not only does the ace win a trick in its own right, it can also upgrade the chance that an accompanying king makes a trick from half-a-chance into a certainty.

Now try:

The Daily Telegraph Easy Guide to Acol Bridge

Clearly there are three tricks available as you can arrange for the three big cards to be played to different tricks. Note there are now 9 points in the suit and 3 tricks. The relationship, 3 points = 1 trick, that holds good on average is precisely accurate here.

You now have the top four cards in the suits. So you can make four tricks?

No! If you thought four tricks were available you have forgotten the requirement to follow suit. As there are no trumps you can only win a club trick when a club is led to the trick. And when a club is led you must contribute a club from both hands. So when three club tricks have been played you will have no clubs left in either hand. However you plan it, you must waste two of the big cards together on one trick and your limit is three tricks. If you are not convinced, get a pack of cards, lay out the suit as indicated in the various diagrams, and try the plays described.

We have added the two of clubs to the North hand, a card that would only win a trick if there were no cards left in the suit anywhere else. Yet now the possession of the top four cards in the suit does guarantee us four tricks, provided we are careful not to waste two together.

If you want to 'run' four tricks in the suit one after the other, you would also have to be careful about the order in which you played the big cards. Remember that the card that wins one trick determines which hand leads to the next trick. Try it out and you will find that you MUST use the king and jack (but in either order) on the first two rounds of the suit contributing the three and two from dummy. That will leave the lead in the South hand with just the four left and the ace and queen in dummy. When you lead the four the trick will be won in the North hand, the right place to be in order to play the fourth winner and discard a loser from the South hand.

Turn the jack into a small card and then check under what circumstances you might still make four tricks having:

You could play your three sure winners (king, ace and queen) on the first three rounds of the suit leaving the lead in dummy. Then, if by chance, each opponent originally held three of the six missing cards, all the opponents' cards in the suit would be gone and your last card, though small, would be a winner. You have benefited from a lucky 3-3 *break* of the unseen cards. Had one opponent held four or more cards in that suit then he would still have a card to beat yours.

So now you begin to see how, for declarer, the sight of both his own hand and dummy hand allows declarer to plan how to make the maximum number of tricks in each suit. Next look at this suit:

How many tricks should you make?

Answer: Three. You have four big cards in the suit (king, queen, jack and ten) and each time the suit is led you can arrange to play them on different tricks. One opponent has the ace to beat one of those four tricks, but having used his ace it has gone and your side must win the remaining tricks in the suit.

You may be thinking 'but when the opponent plays his ace and wins the trick he will choose what suit to lead to the next trick.' So would you think it a good idea to play this suit early in the play of a hand or later on?

Most beginners do precisely the wrong thing here. Reluctant to lose the lead they play other suits first where they have immediate winners. Later, when eventually they get around to playing this suit, they have no winners left in the other suits to regain the lead and may make no club tricks at all. The correct technique is to get rid of the opponents' ace of clubs while you have winners in the other suits to regain the lead. Then you can make three tricks in the suit. So this suit should be led early in the play.

At last you are ready for a full hand. As declarer, when dummy goes down you can see 27 cards. Why 27? You can see your own 13, the 13 visible in dummy and the one card already played to trick one by the opponent to your left. Suppose your contract is to make nine tricks with no trumps. (As we say how many tricks more than six we must make, this contract would be 3NT).

This is what you can see sitting South:

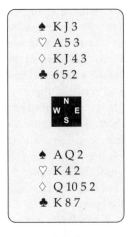

Lead by West: ♠10

Note your side has a total of 26 high-card points (14 in the South hand, and 12 in the North), so the expectation is that you should be able to make 9 tricks (3 points = 1 trick again).

Form a plan to win nine tricks. Decide how many tricks you expect to make in each suit, and in which order you would plan to play the suits.

Looking at each suit in turn this should be your conclusion. The spade suit, though it has the four top cards available, will actually only provide three tricks as there are only three spades in each hand. The heart suit will provide exactly two tricks and no more. The diamond suit will provide exactly three tricks, but you need to drive out the opponent's ace in order to obtain these. The club suit is the one we looked at earlier. You have half a chance of making the king provided you lead from the hand opposite the king (i.e. North) and if East plays low, put on the king, hoping that East has the ace (if West has the ace and beats the king, bad luck!).

Having won the *opening* spade lead, which suit should you play at trick two?

It should be diamonds. You need to drive out the ace, whilst you have winners in the other three suits to regain the lead when the diamond trick is lost to the ace. It would be a bad error to play the two winning hearts before touching diamonds, because when you eventually played a diamond the opponent who won the trick might well have winning hearts to play.

If the opponent who has the ace of diamonds does not play it on the first round, keep playing diamonds until he does. Suppose that opponent, when he wins, chooses to play another spade. Win this and then you can safely *cash* the remaining diamond tricks without setting up any diamond tricks for them. An exception would arise if, on the first diamond trick one opponent proved to have no cards in the suit. That means the other opponent actually holds all the missing five cards in the suit. When four rounds of the suit have been played, that opponent would still have one left, and it would then be a winner, however small.

After diamonds, what suit would you tackle?

Answer: Try to make a club trick with the king. You can see three spade tricks, two heart tricks and have set up three diamond tricks, a total of eight tricks. But you need nine for the contract and must take a risk to make that club trick to fulfil the contract. So arrange to win the last diamond trick in dummy, and then lead a club from that hand, the North hand. If East plays the ace, play a small card from the South hand. Whatever East chooses to play next, win and now you have nine tricks in sight, cash all your winners to make the contract.

When you first lead the club from dummy, if East plays low, don't make the error of assuming he does not have the ace. If West held the ace your king is dead whatever you do, so play on the positive assumption that East has the ace, even though you don't know he has it. East might well play low despite holding the ace. He will have another chance to make it later, and maybe hoping to kill a bigger card of yours with it.

So, after East plays low on the first club, you must nevertheless play the king and hope. If West beats the king with the ace, bad luck! Your contract will now surely fail, but at least you gave it your best shot. If the king of clubs actually wins the trick, you can see your way to nine tricks and your contract. Take all the winners, and don't mind a jot if you lose the rest. Your key target has been achieved.

Having established the basics of card play with no trumps, look next at a contract with a trump suit, and see what difference that makes.

The unique property of the trump suit is that a trump can win a trick even when some other suit was led to the trick. To do this the hand that wins the trick with a trump must have no cards in the suit led, else it would have to obey the rule of following suit and could not play a trump.

You can then make trumps one at a time, rather than use up two trumps to one trick as you must do when a trump is led. Look at this holding in three suits when it is your lead with six tricks left to play:

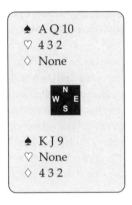

If the contract was no trumps and it was your lead but the opponents still held cards in each suit, then you would be limited to three spade tricks. The opponents would win the rest. But if spades are trumps you can actually make SIX spade tricks! Not if you lead trumps, of course, for then you must follow suit with a spade from each hand. Instead you must take advantage of the fact that you have no diamonds in the North hand and no hearts in the South hand. That means you can lead a diamond from the South hand, and having none in the North hand, can play any card. Of course you should choose to play a trump, and as the opponents have no bigger trump to play, that trump must win the trick. The lead is now in the North hand and you next lead a heart. Having none of those in the South hand, again you are able to choose to play a trump and win the trick. And so you continue on your merry way, making all the remaining six tricks.

The word *ruff* is used to describe playing a trump to a trick when it was not a trump that was led to the trick. The technique above of doing this several times one trick after the other is called *cross-ruffing*. Note that the lead changes hands each time, as a ruff must be won in a different hand to the hand that led to the trick.

Note also that the opponents may also 'get a ruff' if one of them has a trump but no card in the suit led by declarer. To prevent this happening, a declarer who has many more trumps than the opponents and the best cards in the trump suit, normally starts by removing the opponents' small trumps before they do any harm by ruffing declarer's winners. The technique is called *drawing trumps*.

Suppose, as declarer, you have nine trumps between you and dummy. The opponents have the remaining four trumps. If you lead trumps, the opponents must follow suit, and when you have seen them contribute their four trumps, you stop leading trumps, as the opponents have none left to do any damage. You can turn your attention to other suits, and perhaps make your trumps separately later on by ruffing.

A further use to the trump suit is to prevent an opponent who is on lead winning tricks in another suit when you have no cards of that suit. Suppose an opponent won the last trick and now leads a winner in a suit that is not trumps. If the contract is 'no-trumps' he would win the trick. But if there is a trump suit and you had no cards in the suit led you could play a trump and win the trick, thereby also regaining the choice of what to lead next. The technique of keeping back some trumps for late in the play to regain the lead lost to an opponent is called *retaining trump control*.

Now you know the three key trump techniques of drawing trumps, ruffing and retaining trump control it is time to look at a full deal. Look at these two hands:

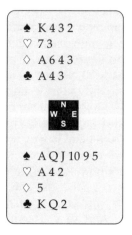

Lead by West: ♣J

Your contract is to make twelve tricks with spades as trumps ('Six Spades' or 6♠). This is a *small slam* with a big reward in the scoring if you fulfil it. Can you see the way to 12 tricks?

Look at each suit in turn. Even if there were no trumps you can count six spade tricks. You have all the big spades but would not make more tricks than you have cards in the longer holding of the suit. You can also count one heart trick, one diamond trick, and three club tricks, but no hope of any more in these suits. This is a total of 11 tricks. You need one more for the contract. That extra trick must come from a ruff, making use of the extra power of the trump suit.

To obtain a ruff you must have no cards of the suit led to the trick in the hand opposite. Where can you do this? Not in clubs, as you have three clubs in each hand. What about in diamonds? Ah! After playing a diamond to the ace and winning the trick you could lead a small diamond from dummy and, having none in your own hand, win that trick with a trump. But hang on a minute. You have won one trick with a trump but now have only five trumps left in the South hand, a total of six trump tricks, exactly the same as when there are no trumps. You have won a trick with a small trump, it is true, but have not gained a trick.

What you need to do is to make a ruff in the North hand, with the fewer trumps, thereby still making the six trump tricks available in the South hand. Then you will win SEVEN tricks with trumps.

Can you do this? Yes, in hearts. But in order to create the position of having no hearts in the North hand you must first play TWO heart tricks. One can be won with the ace, but the other must be lost. However, your contract allows you to lose one trick and still make twelve. So that losing heart trick must be the only trick lost.

Before you play anything else you should draw the opponents' trumps. You have ten, so they have three. Win the club lead, and start by leading trumps. If they both follow suit to the first trump trick, two of their three trumps have gone. One remains and draw that with one more lead of trumps. Now the opponents have no more trumps left, STOP playing trumps. If you kept on playing trumps you would leave dummy with no trumps to ruff that third heart trick.

Having drawn trumps it would do no harm to take the club tricks and the ace of diamonds, but those tricks can be taken later if you wish. The next key task is to play two rounds of hearts, for example, by playing the ace to win one heart trick and then another heart that must be lost to an opponent. Whatever that opponent plays next – say, a diamond – win the trick. Now get the lead into the South hand, say by playing a club and putting the king on. When the lead is in the South hand lead the last heart from that hand. The opponents have bigger hearts left to beat it, but you now have no hearts in the dummy, and can play a trump (ruff) to win the trick. As the rest of your tricks are obvious winners you could even show our cards to the opponents and *claim* the rest.

You made one heart trick, one diamond trick, three club tricks, six trump tricks by the power of the trumps in the South hand, and the crucial twelfth trick by way of a heart ruff in dummy. Well done, slam made!

Summary for The Basics of Card Play

- As declarer, before playing from dummy, try to estimate how many tricks you will win in each suit.

- When leading to a trick you must follow suit from the hand opposite, but you can plan how to avoid crashing high cards together. When there are no trumps you can never make more tricks in any suit than the longest holding in either hand.

- The card that wins one trick determines who leads to the next trick, so the order in which you play the winners is important. The lead needs to be in the right place at the right time.

- A common mistake among beginners is to 'cash' all immediate winners first, leaving no means of regaining the lead when an early trick is lost in a suit where there are winners to be set up. Instead, you should set up ('establish') winners in suits where they are not immediately available while you still have winners elsewhere.

- One of the most important techniques in bridge is the finesse. This is an attempt to win a trick with a card that is not the highest by leading that suit from the hand opposite the high card. The opponent who plays second to the trick has to decide what to play before you. Even if that opponent does not play the higher card, it is often right to assume he holds it, because should it lie with the other opponent your lower card has no chance of winning whatever you do.

- When there is a trump suit there are three key aspects of play: drawing trumps, taking ruffs, and retaining trump control. Drawing trumps means leading them until the opponents have none left, thus removing the danger that their trumps might beat one your winners in other suits. Taking ruffs means being able to lead a losing card in a non-trump suit and, because there are no cards of that suit in the other hand, play a trump and win the trick. Thus you score some of your trumps separately rather than two trumps at a time as when drawing trumps. Aim to take your ruffs in the hand with the fewer trumps so as to preserve the longer trump holding to win tricks in the normal way. If you lose the lead to an opponent who has winners to play, you will want to have some trumps left to play on these winners in order to regain the lead. If drawing trumps would leave you with trumps in only one hand you will have to take your ruffs first, but the more trumps you have the more likely it will be that you should draw trumps first and then go for your ruffs.

Exercise for Basics of Card Play

Q1 Suppose you wished to make two tricks with this holding in a suit:

How could you use a finesse to win a trick with the queen, even though one opponent has the king to beat that card?

A1 With the South hand on lead, lead the suit and watch West's card. If he plays the king beat it with the ace, and then make the queen for the second trick. If West plays a small card, try the queen. If West held the king the queen will win the trick and the ace provides the second trick. If East held the king and beats the queen, bad luck! The finesse failed and you make only one trick, the ace, after regaining the lead.

Q2 How many tricks would you expect to make with the holding below? Assume you enough winners in the other suits to regain the lead after losing a trick:

A2 One. You have three big cards to play, the queen, jack and ten, and will play them on different tricks. The opponents have two big cards to beat them (the ace and king) and can also arrange to play them on different tricks, so they will win two of the three tricks and you one.

Q3 In a no-trump contract is there any layout of the unseen cards that would prevent you making five tricks in the suit below, and when would you discover that was the case?

♠ A Q J 3 2

♠ K 5 4

A3 There are five cards missing in the suit. If one opponent held all five of these (a very unlucky 5-0 break) then that opponent would have a winner after you had played your four big cards. You would discover 'the bad news' on the first round of the suit. One opponent would not follow suit, proving he held none, and you know at once the other opponent not only held all five missing cards in the suit, but also that he 'guards' the fifth round.

Q4 How would you play this deal to make twelve tricks with clubs as trumps?

♠ A 3 2
♡ 7 5 4
◇ A 3
♣ K J 8 4 3

♠ K Q J 4
♡ K Q
◇ 4 2
♣ A Q 10 5 2

Lead by West: ◇K

A4 You have five trump tricks, one diamond trick, four spade tricks and can set up one heart trick, total 11, one too few. The twelfth trick must come from a ruff, but how? Win the diamond lead with the ace, draw trumps, noting when all three of the opponents' trumps are gone, then stop playing trumps and cash the four spades throwing the small diamond from dummy. Now, because there are no diamonds in the dummy, you can ruff your losing diamond and play on hearts. You still have trumps left to regain the lead and make your heart trick.

Q5 How would play a contract to make ten tricks with spades as trumps, if you held these cards:

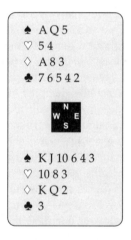

Lead by West: ◇10

A5 You have nine winners easily available (six spade tricks and three diamond tricks) but need one more. This can come from ruffing a heart in dummy. You cannot afford to draw trumps first as this might take three rounds and dummy would have no trumps left to take care of the third heart. So having won the lead you play on hearts, knowing you are going to lose two tricks. Repeat this idea until you have obtained the heart ruff. Then draw trumps and play your other winners.

3
Starting Bidding

The bidding actually precedes the play of the deal. It is an *auction* starting with the dealer going round to the left. Each player has the opportunity to name a contract for his side, providing that contract is higher than any preceding contract named. A player not wishing to name a higher contract may Pass.

(The phrase 'No Bid' is also commonly used in some countries, including England and Wales, instead of Pass, but as the word 'Pass' is used throughout the world we will use it in this book. Whatever your group of players does, it should always do the same, i.e. it would be wrong sometimes to say Pass and sometimes to say No Bid.)

The bidding continues round the table, maybe several times but all four players must have at least one chance to name a contract, until three consecutive players Pass. This ends the bidding and the final contract named becomes the contract for the play. The side that named the contract is the declaring side. Declarer is the member of that side who first suggested the denomination of the final contract. Note this is not necessarily the same player who made the final bid, it might be declarer's partner who actually made the final bid. The defender to declarer's left makes the *opening* lead and then dummy is faced.

If none of the four players is prepared to name a contract (i.e. the bidding went: Pass Pass Pass Pass) then the bidding has finished without a contract and there is no play for that deal. In rubber bridge you would simply get on with the next deal. In duplicate you would record a score of zero for both sides and that deal would still go to the other tables where someone may decide to bid on a hand that was Passed at your table.

How are contracts named?

Put long-windedly, a player is making this statement: 'When it comes to the play, my partner and I, between us, will win at least x of the 13 tricks, provided y is trumps.' That is why it is called a contract, like a legally binding undertaking. Of course, you don't have to make the long statement every time, you only have to specify the x and y, the level and denomination of the contract. The level stated is the number of tricks more than six, and the denomination is what you want as trumps. Thus when a player says: 'One Heart,' i.e. 1♡, this is the short way of saying: 'When it comes to the play, my partner and I will win at least one trick more than six, i.e. at least seven tricks with hearts as trumps.' A contract of 3NT is an undertaking to win at least nine tricks with no trumps.

The auction must go upwards. 'Upwards' means either the level

---

must be higher than the previous level named, or the level can be the same provided the denomination named is senior to the previous denomination. The seniority of the suits is alphabetical order starting with clubs as the junior suit, then diamonds, hearts and spades as the senior suit. No-trumps is the top denomination. So the ranking of the 35 possible contracts (seven levels and five denominations in each level) is this. starting with the junior contract, 1♣, and ending with the top one, 7NT:

1♣	1◇	1♡	1♠	1NT
2♣	2◇	2♡	2♠	2NT
3♣	3◇	3♡	3♠	3NT
4♣	4◇	4♡	4♠	4NT
5♣	5◇	5♡	5♠	5NT
6♣	6◇	6♡	6♠	6NT
7♣	7◇	7♡	7♠	7NT

In addition to the 35 contracts and Pass, there are two other legal calls, *double* and *redouble*. These do not change the contract, only the scoring of the contract, so further mention is left until we cover scoring in detail.

In the auction you can miss out as many contracts as you like. The auction is presented in a diagram with West always on the left. The first call indicates the dealer. Look at this auction:

West	North	East	South
	Pass	1♡	1♠
2♡	2♠	4♡	All Pass

Here North was the dealer and, deciding not to name a contract, Passed. East *opened* the bidding for his side with 1♡, a contract to make seven tricks with hearts as trumps. South *overcalled* 1♠, a permissible bid because spades are senior to hearts, so South could keep the bidding at the same level. Had South wanted clubs as trumps, the lowest bid he could have made would be 2♣ because clubs are junior to hearts and so the level must increase. West *responded* 2♡ to his partner's opening, raising the level of the contract to eight tricks. Had the next three players Passed, then 2♡ would have become the final contract. West would have named the final contract but East, who first suggested hearts as trumps, would be the declarer.

However, the bidding continued with North *raising* South's overcall, and then East *jumped* to 4♡, which became the final contract. All Pass means the next three players Passed ending the auction. East is the declarer as he bid hearts before West. His contract is to win at least ten of the 13 tricks. The player on declarer's left, South, must lead to the first trick, and then West will face his hand as dummy, with hearts on West's right, i.e. declarer's left. North and South must then try to prevent East making his contract. The target of North-South is therefore to win four tricks, as if they do so, they will leave East with at most nine, and his contract will have failed.

If the contract succeeds, East-West have a plus score on the deal, North-South the same score but minus. If the contract fails, North-South have a plus score, East-West an equal minus.

Why, you might be thinking, did East unnecessarily jump to 4♡, giving himself a more ambitious contract to fulfil? The answer lies with the scoring, a subject covered in a later chapter. All you need to know at the moment is that the more ambitious the contract, the higher the reward the declaring side will get in the score, provided the contract is made. So one skill in bidding is to judge how high you can go and still fulfil the contract when it comes to the play.

The most ambitious contract is the grand slam, i.e. a contract to make all 13 tricks, rare and difficult as the defenders only have to take one trick to beat it. Next down is the small slam, a contract to make at least 12 of the 13 tricks. The scoring rewards a grand slam significantly more than the small slam, because if a side bids the grand slam and fails by one trick, it has lost the chance to score the reward for the small slam.

Next down from the small slam in terms of bonus in the scoring come what are called *game contracts*. They differ according to the denomination and are: 3NT, 4♡, 4♠, 5♣ and 5♢.

When scoring is covered in detail you find the scoring of contracts with hearts or spades as trumps is identical but worth more than diamonds and clubs. Hearts and spades are called the *major* suits. Diamonds and clubs (the scoring for their contracts is identical) are, no surprise, called the *minor* suits. All you need to remember at this stage is that game in no-trumps is nine tricks, game in a major suit is ten tricks, and game in a minor suit is 11 tricks.

The contracts worth less than game are called 'part-games' or, more usually, *part-scores*. A declarer in a part-score contract does not score the bonus for game even when he makes enough tricks for game. That explains why East, in the auction shown earlier, went to 4♡. He was expecting to make at least 10 tricks, but not 12 (or he might have tried for the small slam) and wanted the game bonus.

Roughly speaking, bridge scoring is designed to make it worthwhile for you to go for a contract with a higher scoring bonus, provided you have better than half a chance of making the higher contract. Even if East thought he could make precisely 11 tricks with hearts as trumps there would be no advantage in bidding to that level rather than the game of 4♡ as the next higher bonus is the small slam where he would have to contract for 12 tricks. Note that when the contract is 4♡ East does not have to make precisely 10 tricks in the play, only at least 10 tricks. If he makes any *overtricks* the scoring gives him a small reward for that, but if he gets two overtricks, and makes 12 tricks, he does not get the small slam bonus as the bonus only arises when you both bid for and make 12 tricks.

How did East come to the conclusion that his side could win 10 tricks in the play, given that he had not seen his partner's hand? Answer: all the players make deductions about a hand that they cannot see from the bids the owner of the hand makes.

For example, we will advise you to open the bidding for your side if you have a hand that is something like a trick better than an average hand (a more precise definition of this in a moment). So when North Passed originally all the other three players, including partner South, would deduce that North's hand was not better than average. By contrast, East did open the bidding, so the other three players deduce his hand is better than average.

There is no Law against a player bluffing. North could legally Pass with a good hand just as a poker player might 'check' with a good hand planning to raise later, or East might open with a weak hand, but at bridge bluffing is rarely a success. You have a partner, and when he is misled the disaster that befalls you is usually far greater than any reward you may reap for having fooled the opponents. So we will assume for the great bulk of this book that no player is bluffing (in bridge the word is *psyching*).

You can make a further deduction from East's opening bid of 1♡. Why did he suggest hearts as trumps rather than spades, diamonds or clubs?

The answer is that he has *more* hearts than he has cards in any other suit, or more precisely, that he has 'no suit longer' than hearts. (He might have another suit with as many cards as he has in hearts.) In choosing a trump suit it is quantity that matters much more than quality. Say you held in spades A K Q, and in hearts 6 5 4 3 2 it would be hearts you wanted as trumps, not spades. The top spades will probably take tricks whatever the trump suit, but the extra hearts you have will prove useful as trumps when you run out of diamonds or clubs and play a small heart and win the trick.

If East has no suit with more cards in it than his heart suit, what is the minimum number of hearts he must have?

The answer is 4. Suppose East held three spades, three hearts, three diamonds, and three clubs. That would be only 12 cards. Impossible! The thirteenth card must make one of the suits into four cards or longer. *Every* bridge hand has a 4-card or longer suit.

We are going to teach you a method of bidding, by far the most popular in Britain, in which the opening bidder is assumed not to have any suit with more cards in it than the one he bid first. The *system* is called *Acol*, after the Acol Bridge Club in Acol Road, North London, where the system was first devised in the 1930s. The Laws of Bridge do not define what players can deduce from the bids. A partnership can agree before the game starts what their bids imply. The Laws say only that such agreements must not be secret. If a partnership has an agreement as to what a particular bid implies, the opponents should also be aware of this agreement. A coherent set of agreements about what bids mean, such as Acol, is a bidding *system.*

There are systems popular in, say, the USA and France where East may open 1♣ with fewer than four cards in the suit, and will therefore have a longer suit elsewhere ('The Prepared Club'). There are systems popular in, for example, Italy and China where the opening bid of 1♣ might promise that the player has a strong hand generally, rather than length in clubs ('The Strong Club'). These are not the methods taught in this book. Acol is the world's most *natural* bidding system in the sense that you open the bidding with the suit where you have the most cards.

When East opens 1♡ using Acol the other three players deduce the following three things: East has a better than average hand, has at least four cards in the heart suit, and has no suit longer than hearts. So if, by chance, West also has at least four hearts, he knows the partnership has at least eight hearts between them. Without having seen his partner's hand he can deduce that hearts is a satisfactory trump suit. When West raised East to 2♡ he was implying: 'We have located a suit in which we have at least eight trumps, and working on the assumption you have a minimum opening hand I reckon we can win eight tricks with hearts as trumps.' Armed with this information East, holding a hand much better than a minimum opening, judged that the partnership could make 10 tricks, and so bid the contract of 4♡.

We must now be much more precise about how to judge whether you have a hand worth opening the bidding. First count your high-card points. You already know the pack has 40 HCP, and there are four players sitting round the table, so on average each player will have 10 points. You also know that each extra 3 points you hold should win you one extra trick in the play, so if you held 13 HCP you could assess your hand as being one trick better than average.

Note that when you open with a bid at the one level, you are not saying 'I will win 7 tricks when it comes to the play', but 'my partner and I between us will make at least 7 tricks when it comes to the play.' You start by making a reasonable assumption about the unseen hands, including partner's, until you have the evidence to be more accurate. For example, if you have 13 points, then the remaining 27 points are shared between the other three players, and initially your best guess would be to expect each of them to hold 9 points.

But it not just high cards that increase the trick-taking potential of a bridge hand. Long suits are also good news. Suppose your holding in spades is A K Q J 2: the two of spades in its own right would not win a trick, but when you get the lead in a contract where spades are trumps or there are no trumps you can anticipate leading out your big spades first with the opponents following suit. By the time you get round to leading the two of spades the opponents probably have no spades left and your two of spades wins the trick. The *length* of your spade suit increased the chance the small cards became winners. If your suit was J 5 4 3 2 you would be less confident, but even then, if your partner had four cards in the same suit, it is probable your small cards could be promoted into winners.

Long suits increase your trick-taking potential so we ask you to upgrade your hand in terms of points when you first see your hand, adding one point for a 5-card suit, 2 points for a 6-card suit, 3 points for a 7-card suit and so on. The total point count defines the *strength* of your hand (in terms of trick-taking potential). If you held two 5-card suits you would add 1 point for each.

Note this is nothing to do with scoring, and there is nothing about counting your points in the Laws of Bridge. This is merely a method of assessing how many tricks you will take in the play. The valuation of high-card points (A=4, K=3, Q=2, J=1) is universal, but there is no such worldwide agreement about how to assess the value of long suits. The number of cards you have in each suit defines the *shape* of your hand and good bridge players use their experience to judge how shape affects their trick-taking potential. Those starting out have no such experience, and so we give you this evaluation of upgrading by 1 point for every card more than four in one suit. This is a good guide to use until you have the experience to evaluate your hand shape more accurately.

Curiously, short suits can also be helpful, but their value cannot be assessed at once. A short suit is one where you have fewer than three cards: a two-card suit is called a *doubleton,* a suit with only one card in it is a *singleton,* and a suit where you have no cards is a *void.*

Suppose you had a singleton club. If your partner insisted that clubs was trumps this singleton would be bad news. If the final contract was no-trumps, the singleton club would be a worry (the opponents might be able to make several tricks in the suit). This worry would be significantly reduced if you knew that clubs was your partner's longest suit. The singleton would not be good news, but it would not necessarily be a negative factor.

But if you had located another suit, say hearts as the trump suit in which you had eight or more cards, now the singleton club becomes good news, in two possible ways. An opponent with the ace and king of clubs may think he has two winners, but you know on the second round of clubs you will have no clubs left and will be able to play a trump and win the trick. Similarly suppose your partner has a singleton diamond. Then when you are out of clubs and partner is out of diamonds you will be able to cross-ruff, making your trumps singly, rather than needing to use up two trumps at a time as when following suit to a trump lead.

There is no worldwide agreement on evaluating short suits, but the method used in this book is:

Give no value to short suits until you know your side has a satisfactory trump suit (defined to be one with 8 cards or more between the two hands). When you discover such a trump fit, upgrade your hand by assigning this value to the short suits:

For a doubleton outside the trump suit, upgrade your point count by 1;
For a singleton outside the trump suit, upgrade your point count by 2;
For a void outside the trump suit, upgrade by 3 points.

Initially you counted only high-card points (HCP) and long-suit points. If you had a total of 13 points you would be a full trick better than average and would have a clear-cut opening bid. However it must be said that bridge players these days open many, maybe most, 12-point hands. For example, you hold:

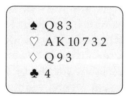

You have 11 HCP and 2 long-suit points (for the 6-card heart suit) – a clear-cut though minimum-type opening of 1♡. If you changed the queen of diamonds into the jack, you would have 10 HCP and 2 long-suit points, a hand that many bridge players, but not all, would open 1♡. If you changed the queen of diamonds into the 10, you would have 9 HCP and 2-long-suit points, a hand that few players would open 1♡ but some might. We advise against opening a hand with fewer than 12 points (HCP plus long-suit points) and advise you do open all hands with 13 points or more. Beginners may well be advised not to open on 12 points, but most players do, so we will generally follow that practice in this book.

Until much later in the book all opening bids will be at the one level.

In Acol openings at the two level require 20 points or more (half the points in the pack). So when a player opens at the one level his point count range (HCP + long-suit) is somewhere between the absolute minimum of 12, and 19.

Now go back to the auction given earlier. Here is a reminder:

West	North	East	South
	Pass	1♡	1♠
2♡	2♠	4♡	All Pass

Suppose this is East's bridge hand:

♠ 2
♡ A Q J 8 5 2
◊ K Q 9 6
♣ K 9

When East picked up his cards, he would count 15 HCP and 2 long-suit points (for the 6-card heart suit), a total of 17. As this is significantly better than average, and in the range 13-19, he would clearly open with one of his longest suit, namely 1♡. Partner raised to 2♡ hearts, indicating West knew the partnership had eight hearts (East actually now knows they have at least 10) and that opposite a minimum opening West expects the partnership to win eight of the 13 tricks.

East now upgrades his hand by two points for the singleton spade. This holding is obviously good news as it prevents the opponents making more than one trick in spades. East might also upgrade by one point for the doubleton club (though that is less clear-cut an improvement). But as East now counts 19 or even 20 points, i.e. at least seven points more than a minimum opening he expects to make two tricks more than West reckoned. Hence East's raise to 4♡ in the expectation that he will make 10 tricks and get the bonus for bidding and making the game contract.

Look at this auction where only one side is bidding:

West	North	East	South
1♠	Pass	3♠	Pass
4♠	All Pass		

West was in the range 12-19 points with no suit longer than spades. East raised as he held four or more spades and knew the partnership had eight spades or more between them. When East raised, as he had found the trump suit, he was able to indicate the strength of his hand at the same time by how high he raised. The Acol principle is that East should start by making a pessimistic assumption about West's hand, namely that West has a minimum opening, but then bid as boldly as he can. He leaves West to go on higher if West actually has a hand that is better than a minimum (remember three extra points garner one extra trick).

By that neat three-step scheme the partnership arrives at the right level without either member of the side having seen partner's hand. Here are two hands that would fit the auction given above:

First West, holding:

♠ A J 10 3 2
♡ K Q 5 4
◊ K 10 2
♣ 3

West initially counts 13 HCP and 1 long-suit point, total 14, a sound opening bid, and opens one of his longest suit, 1♠. When East raises to 3♠, West upgrades his hand by 2 points for the singleton club, making a total of 16. As this is at least 3 points better than a minimum opening West can certainly go on to 4♠ to try for the game bonus.

How did East, the *responder* to West's opening, decide to jump to 3♠ rather than the more cautious 2♠ or very bold immediate 4♠?

The Acol principle is very simple. For each level higher East bids, he is promising one extra trick, i.e. three extra points. So if you can work out the strength of one particular raise by East, the rest will follow easily.

When you were playing MiniBridge we taught you to expect that the partnership would need, say, 27 points to make 9 tricks (we divided the point count by 3 to arrive at expected tricks). But bridge players have learned to be a little more ambitious. In a trump contract declarer has a slight advantage over the defenders because declarer instructs dummy what to play. If declarer's plan involves dummy playing a heart when on lead, declarer simply tells dummy to play a heart. Life is not so easy for the opponents. One defender may be desperately wishing partner would lead a club, but the Laws forbid any communication between them other than by the bids made and the cards played. Two minds are not greater than one when communication is restricted.

Declarer's advantage is not so great when there are no trumps because the defenders are given one advantage that is particularly important in no-trumps, namely the lead to the first trick. Many no-trump contracts are a race between the two sides to set up their best suit first. If the defender on lead hits declarer's weak spot at once, that may prove decisive.

This leads to the conclusion that in a trump contract you should be one trick more ambitious than the basic rule of 3 points = 1 trick. Most teachers estimate that 27 points is sufficient to justify reaching 4♡ or 4♠ (game in a major suit), that 30 points will suffice for 5♣ or 5♢ (game in a minor suit), and that 33 points is enough to bid a small slam. For a grand slam, where the defence need only one trick to defeat it, you need to be on more secure ground and we advise the partnership having 37 or even 38 points (remember these points include HCP, long-suit points and short-suit points).

Return to the question of how high East should raise when West opens 1♠, and East has four cards in the same suit. East starts by assuming West has a minimum opening, say 13 points, but, having made that pessimistic assumption, then raises as boldly as he dares. Hence East should have about 11 points to raise to 3♠ (the partnership has 24 points, enough to make 9 tricks in a trump contract). If East held 14 points he would raise to 4♠, and if he held only 8 points he would raise to 2♠. Of course he may not hold exactly the right number of points. Each raise has a 3-point range, namely 7-9, 10-12, 13-15. In real life bridge players hate Passing when they have 4-card support for partner, so we also advise raising to Two of opener's suit with as few as six points. There are two reasons for this. Firstly when the opener upgrades his hand on discovering the trump fit, he might have as many as 21 points, which with our six will provide enough for game. Secondly, even if opener has an absolute minimum and we fail by one trick in 2♠, we need not worry, as the opponents have more than half the points, and could have made a contract of their own.

To summarise, when responder has 4-card support for opener, he should raise to the following level:

with: 0-5 points   Pass, not raising at all (you are high enough already);
6-9 points   raise to Two;
10-12 points   raise to Three;
13-15 points   raise to Four.

This pattern could even be extended. For a beginner who, as responder, held 4-card or better support for the suit opened by partner, it would make sense:

with: 16-18 points   to raise to Five (opener might have enough to go on to slam);

    19-23 points   to raise direct to the small slam (Six), and

    24 points or more   raise all the way to the grand slam (Seven)!

But there are more accurate ways of investigating slams. These are described later in the book.

Here is a typical hand to raise partner's opening 1♠ to 3♠:

♠ K Q 6 5
♡ 6 3
◊ A 9 3 2
♣ 10 6 3

When you pick up this hand you count 9 HCP and no long-suit points. When you hear partner open 1♠ you at once know the partnership has eight or more spades, and that spades is a satisfactory trump suit. You therefore upgrade your hand by 1 point for the doubleton heart, making 10 in total, and stretch to 3♠. You may recall partner went on to 4♠ holding:

♠ A J 10 3 2
♡ K Q 5 4
◊ K 10 2
♣ 3

4♠ on the two hands is a perfectly sensible contract, despite holding only 22 HCP. You have eight obvious tricks (five trumps, one heart and two diamonds) and can ruff at least one heart in dummy to give you the ninth. The tenth trick might come from an extra ruff, or an extra heart trick, or an extra diamond trick, quite sufficient prospects to justify trying for the game bonus. You expect to lose only one club (you can trump the second round of clubs in the South hand), one heart (the ace) and one diamond (the queen or jack).

West's opening bid of 1♠ had a wide range of strength (12 to 19), whereas East's raise was defining his strength to within one trick (a 3-

point range). The two bids are completely different in character. We call the first type *exploratory* because at the time West was seeking a trump suit and his strength was not closely defined. The second type is called a *limit* bid because the bid placed narrow limits upon the strength of the hand. There is a third category of bid mentioned later in the book called a *convention* when the partnership has a special prior agreement about the meaning of the bid, not obvious from the bid itself.

Before making a bid, or when interpreting a bid by partner, first work out to which category the bid belongs. There is no simple way of remembering whether a bid is a convention, but as we have not yet introduced you to any, you don't have to worry about that yet. What you need to be able to do now is to work out which bid is exploratory and which is limit. Fortunately for beginners there is a simple rule that covers the great majority of cases. It is this:

When a suit is first suggested as trumps the bid is exploratory, other bids (including all no-trump bids) are limit bids.

So, in the auction (putting dashes for the Passes by the other side): 1♠ – 3♠ – 4♠ – Pass only the first bid is exploratory, because it was the first time spades had been suggested as trumps.

The next chapter covers auctions such as 1♡ – 1♠ – 2♡/2♠ – Pass. Here the first two bids are exploratory as first hearts, and then spades were initially suggested as trumps. But the 2♡/2♠ rebid by opener is a limit bid because it is the second time the suit has been mentioned.

The raise in the same suit indicates the trump suit has been found, and the player making the raise can at the same time show their strength, placing partner with the minimum points he has promised so far, but then raising as boldly as is reasonable.

All limit bids can be Passed by partner, but with extra values he may move on. The key question is whether the partnership has the strength to make a higher contract that carries a bigger bonus in the scoring. If so, the partner of the limit bidder goes on, knowing that for each extra 3 points he holds above his minimum the side can make one extra trick. By contrast, whilst the partnership is seeking the trump suit it is necessary to keep the bidding as low as possible and so the players cannot also define their strength accurately as they explore for the trump suit.

The fact that the game bonus only arises when the partnership both bids and makes game gives a particular interest to an auction that starts like this: 1♡ – 2♡ – 3♡. West opens 1♡, East raises to 2♡ showing a trump fit with 6-9 points. West then goes to 3♡, a contract that is more difficult to make than 2♡, but is not enough to get the game bonus. Why should West do this?

A sensible reason is that West thinks there is a chance of obtaining the game bonus by making 4♡. West could have a hand where if East's strength is at the bottom end of the range 6-9, 4♡ would be too ambitious, but if East was at the top end of the range then 4♡ would be a sensible target. West is said to be *inviting* East to go to the game contract if East is at the top end of the range for his bidding so far. East will Pass 3♡ if he has 6 or 7 points, but go on to 4♡ if he has 8 or 9.

Having covered responder raising opener's suit, we now look at responder suggesting no-trumps as the denomination for the contract.

We have said all no-trump bids are limit bids but no-trump contracts may be more difficult for declarer than trump contracts because of the danger that the opening leader hits a weak spot. This is counterbalanced by the fact that the game bonus for no-trumps goes to a nine trick contract, 3NT, whereas the trump suit games are higher.

Responder (the opener's partner) suggests no-trumps with a *balanced* hand that does not have 4-cards in the same suit as the one partner opened. By balanced we mean a roughly equal number of cards in each suit. The most balanced shape is clearly 4-3-3-3, by which we mean you hold one 4-card suit and three suits with three cards each. The next most balanced shape is 4-4-3-2 (this is the most common shape in bridge). Other shapes might be acceptable for no-trump bidding (e.g. with 5-3-3-2 it will depend on whether you prefer to tell partner about the 5-card suit), but for the moment we will concentrate on the first two.

A game contract of 3NT requires 25 or 26 points rather than the 24 that would be sufficient to make three of a suit with an eight-card trump fit. By saying 25 or 26 points for 3NT, we mean a partnership:

with: 26 points or more   should reach game;
        24 points or less   should keep out of game;
        exactly 25 points   3NT has a roughly 50-50 chance of making.

In the latter case it is not a crime either to be in game or a less ambitious contract. Bridge is not an exact science. You may know the side has at least 25 points or more, in which case you would go for game, or conversely, that your side has at most 25 points but perhaps less, in which case you might decide to keep out of game.

In a suit contract you count short-suit points, whereas for no-trump contracts only high-card and long-suit points are evaluated. Short suits are not good news when there are no trumps.

However, as no-trumps is the top denomination exactly the same scheme of point count ranges can be used for responding in no-trumps one level lower than when raising the same suit. In response to an opening bid at the one level, partner, with a balanced hand and fewer than four cards in opener's suit, will respond in no-trumps. The level will depend on responder's strength:

with:
	0-5 points	Pass;
	6-9 points	respond 1NT;
	10-12 points	respond 2NT;
	13-15 points	respond 3NT.

In the following examples, West opens 1♡. Holding the following hands, East's response is:

(a)	(b)	(c)
♠ J 9 3	♠ Q 10 3	♠ A J 9
♡ 8 4 2	♡ 10 4	♡ 7 3
◇ A Q 7 3	◇ A J 9 3	◇ A 10 9 4
♣ 10 8 4	♣ K J 8 2	♣ K Q 9 3
1NT	2NT	3NT

As opener, what should you rebid when partner responds showing a balanced hand?

First decide whether you are happy with that denomination. If so, Pass whenever you know the side does not have enough for the game bonus awarded to 3NT, i.e. when you know your side has at most 25 points or maybe less. By contrast if you know your side has 25 points or more raise to 3NT.

When the response is the 4-point range 6-9, and the opener has 17-18, he is in doubt about whether to go 3NT, but can sit on the fence by raising to 2NT. Responder, realising that opener did not know whether to Pass or go 3NT, treats the raise as an invitation to go 3NT. Responder accepts if he is in the upper range for his previous bid, but rejects the invitation if at the bottom end, i.e. with 6 or 7 points responder Passes opener's raise to 2NT, but with 8 or 9 points responder moves on to 3NT.

When responder shows a balanced hand, you, as opener, can assume partner has two or three cards in your suit. With a 6-card suit the partnership has at least eight cards in the suit, and you bid it again to have it as trumps. As this is the second mention of that suit, the rebid is a limit bid, not an exploring bid. A rebid of the suit at the lowest possible level (the two level) implies you do not think there is a chance of game. By contrast, any jump bid in the suit would imply game might be on.

For example: West opens 1♡ (exploratory, 12-19 points, no suit longer than hearts). East responds 1NT (6-9 with fewer than four hearts). Now opener, with six hearts and enough to make game opposite 8 or 9 points, should bid 3♡, *invitational*. With six hearts and enough to make game opposite 6 or 7 points, bid 4♡.

Summary of Starting Bidding

- As you sort your cards count your high-card points and then upgrade these for your long suits. Add 1 point for a 5-card suit, 2 points for a 6-card suit, 3 points for a 7-card suit, and, should you hold two 5-card suits, 1 point for each.

- The dealer starts the bidding. In duplicate, as boards are dealt only once but played by several tables, the dealer is marked on the board. Holding less than 12 points dealer should Pass, with 13 points he should always open the bidding. With 12 points, the borderline case, some will open but we suggest a beginner Passes.

- The bidding goes round to the left from the dealer. If the dealer Passed the opponent to his left will have the same decision as to whether to open. If none of the four players opens (i.e. the auction was Pass Pass Pass Pass) then there is no contract for the play. There is a score of zero for both sides, and you move on to the next deal.

- If one player opens, then that player's partner is the responder. Where responder has 4-cards or more in the same suit as the one opened by partner, before bidding, responder upgrades his point count for the short suits in his hand, adding:

for each:	doubleton	1 point;
	singleton	2 points;
	void	3 points

(though it is unlikely you will ever see two voids outside partner's suit!).

- Where the opening is in a minor suit (clubs or diamonds), we explain in the next chapter that responder should seek a major-suit fit if he has four cards in one of them by making an exploratory response in that major. But where responder has no major to bid or the fit found with opener is in a major suit, responder raises the opener to a level determined by responder's point count:

with:	0-5 points	Pass;
	6-9 points	raise to Two;
	10-12 points	raise to Three;
	13-15 points	raise to Four.

- When responder raises, the opener learns the side has found a trump suit with at least eight cards, and the opener therefore also upgrades his point count for the short suits in his hand. For each additional three points above a minimum opening, opener is entitled to raise one trick more. However the next bonus in the scoring only arises if the partnership reaches game. With hearts or spades (the major suits) as trumps, game is a level of Four needing a partnership point count of 27; with clubs or diamonds as trumps (the minor suits) game is Five, needing 30 points. If opener knows the side has 33 points he may try for the small slam bonus by bidding Six.

- If responder does not have 4-card support for opener, he does not upgrade for the short suits. If responder has a balanced hand in shape without 4-card support, he responds in no-trumps using the same ranges as before, but bidding one level lower, namely:

with:		
	0-5 points	Pass;
	6-9 points	respond 1NT;
	10-12 points	respond 2NT;
	13-15 points	respond 3NT.

We explain later that responder needs 9 points to explore at the two level, so with 6-8 points may have to respond 1NT even with a hand that is not particularly balanced.

Opener may Pass if he is happy with the denomination and has not the extra values to justify trying for a contract with a bigger bonus, or he can raise the no-trump response, implying higher ambitions. With a 6-card suit opener could rebid the suit, at a minimum level when he had no higher ambitions, or with a jump bid if he was aiming for a contract with a higher bonus.

Exercise for Starting Bidding

With opponents Passing throughout, and dealer on the left (West in the diagrams below) how should these various pairs of hands be bid? See if you can predict the complete auction by West and East. Each answer, which will include the reasons for the recommended auctions, will be followed by some guidance on how declarer might plan to play the final contract.

Q1

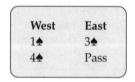

♠ A Q 9 6 3   ♠ K J 4 2
♡ A 10 7 2   ♡ 3
♢ A 10 4   ♢ K 9 5 3 2
♣ 8   ♣ J 6 3

A1 West has 14 HCP and 1 long-suit point (total 15) and opens 1♠. East, with 4-card support for spades, does not seek another trump suit despite holding five diamonds (remember the game contract in spades is only 4♠, whereas the game contract with diamonds as trumps is higher, 5♢). East initially counted 8 HCP and 1 long-suit point, but, having 4-card support for opener, upgrades by two points for the singleton heart. With a total of 11 points, being in the range 10-12, he raises to 3♠. When West hears East raise spades, he upgrades his hand by two points for the singleton club, bringing his count to 17. As West knows the partnership has enough points for game, West goes on to 4♠. The auction has been:

West	East
1♠	3♠
4♠	Pass

THE PLAY: Will West make 4♠? West can expect to lose a diamond trick and one club. In immediate winners, West can only count five spade tricks, one heart and two diamond tricks, but there are two ways to gain the extra two tricks needed. West may get to ruff his losing hearts in dummy, or set up the diamond suit. This way declarer might well make 11 tricks.

The diamond suit has eight cards between the two hands, so the opponents have only five. If these five break 3-2 as they often will, and declarer plays the suit, then dummy will have two of its small diamonds promoted into winners.

♠ ♡ ♢ ♣

Q2

A2 West has 10 HCP and one long-suit point, total 11, and Passes
initially. East has 12 HCP and 1 long-suit point and opens 1♡. When
West hears East open the suit in which he has four cards or more (on
this occasion five), he upgrades his hand by 2 points for the singleton
spade, making a total of 13. West, who Passed originally, now being
in the range 13-15, raises East's 1♡ to 4♡. The auction has been:

West	East
Pass	1♡
4♡	Pass

THE PLAY: Declarer, East, makes at least ten tricks. At worst East loses one
spade, one diamond, and one club, but the finesse position in diamonds
and clubs may well provide an overtrick. Don't forget that declarer on
first obtaining the lead, should draw the opponents' trumps. As East-
West have ten trumps, the opponents only have three. When those three
have gone, declarer must stop leading trumps as later he will wish to
make them separately by ruffing.

♠ ♡ ◇ ♣

Q3

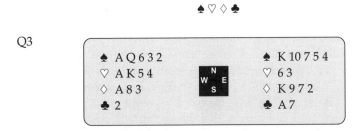

A3 West has 17 HCP and one long-suit point and opens 1♠. East initially
had 10 HCP and one long-suit point, but, on hearing West open 1♠,
East upgrades by one point for each doubleton he holds, bringing
his total strength to 13. East raises to 4♠. West now upgrades his
hand by two points for the singleton club, making a total of 20
points. As East's range is 13-15, West knows the partnership has at
least 33 points and raises to 6♠. The auction has been:

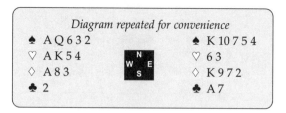

Diagram repeated for convenience

♠ A Q 6 3 2	♠ K 10 7 5 4
♡ A K 5 4	♡ 6 3
◇ A 8 3	◇ K 9 7 2
♣ 2	♣ A 7

West	East
1♠	4♠
6♠	Pass

THE PLAY: The small slam will make easily. Declarer, West, wins any opening lead, draws the opponents' trumps, and then stops playing trumps. Later West ruffs both his small hearts with dummy's remaining trumps. The only losing trick is the third round of diamonds. Declarer makes seven tricks with trumps (five by power and two extra by ruffs), two tricks each in hearts and diamonds, and one in clubs, 12 in total.

♠ ♡ ◇ ♣

Q4

♠ 8 3	♠ 10 4 2
♡ Q J 10 5 3	♡ K 9 4 2
◇ A Q 7	◇ K 6 3
♣ A K 5	♣ Q J 2

A4 West has 16 HCP and 1 long-suit point, and opens 1♡. East has 9 HCP with 4-card support but no long-suit or short-suit points, and raises to 2♡. West upgrades by one point for the doubleton spade, bringing West's total to 18 points. West now has a dilemma. To make 4♡ the side needs 27 points. Responder's range is 6-9, so it remains possible, though not certain, that the side should reach game. West can indicate this by raising to 3♡. East knows West would have no reason to raise unless there was a chance of 4♡, so East should realise he is being invited to move on to 4♡ if he is at the top end of his known range. Thus East, with 6 or 7 points should Pass over 3♡, but with 8 or 9 points, should go on to 4♡. Here East goes on to 4♡. The auction has been:

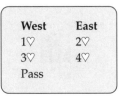

West	East
1♡	2♡
3♡	4♡
Pass	

THE PLAY: 4♡ should make with West losing two spade tricks and the ace of trumps. The main risk is that the opponents may be able to ruff one of West's winners in diamonds or clubs. So when West gains the lead it is right to play on trumps, despite missing the trump ace. The opponents will win and might, if one of them had led a singleton in clubs or diamonds, obtain the ruff that beats West's game. More often, the defenders will not find a ruff, and West will be able to regain the lead and draw the remaining trumps, before safely making the tricks in diamonds and clubs.

♠ ♡ ◇ ♣

Q5

♠ K 9 3		♠ A 10 4
♡ A J 10 3 2	N	♡ 6 4
◇ K J 6	W E	◇ A Q 4 2
♣ A 8	S	♣ J 10 7 3

A5 West has 16 HCP and 1 long-suit point and opens 1♡. East with a balanced hand, fewer than four cards in partner's suit, and a point count in the range 10-12 (he actually has 11) responds 2NT. West, who has a relatively balanced hand himself and has already told East that hearts is his longest suit, knows the partnership has enough points for the game contract of 3NT and raises. The auction has been:

West	East
1♡	2NT
3NT	Pass

THE PLAY: Declarer can see eight easy tricks (two spades, one heart, four diamonds, and the ace of clubs). There are several chances of a ninth trick (spades, hearts and clubs all offer opportunities) and the prospects for making 3NT are much better than 50-50.

♠ ♡ ◇ ♣

♠ A 10 7 5 2　　　　　　　♠ 8 3
♡ K Q 3　　　　　　　　　♡ A J 5 4
◇ A Q 2　　　　　　　　　◇ K 9 4 3
♣ Q 4　　　　　　　　　　♣ J 10 2

A6 West has 17 HCP and 1 long-suit point, and opens 1♠.

East with a balanced hand without 4-card support for spades, and in the range 6-9 points responds 1NT.

West knows that if East is at the bottom end of the range the partnership does not have enough points for 3NT, but if East is at the top end, they do. So West invites by raising to 2NT.

East, at the top end of his range, accepts the invitation by going on to 3NT, the game contract. The auction has been:

West	East
1♠	1NT
2NT	3NT
Pass	

THE PLAY: East can see eight tricks easily available (one spade, four hearts, and three diamonds). There are chances in spades and diamonds for an extra trick, but the club suit, whilst not looking very healthy, actually guarantees a trick for declarer. The opponents have the ace and king, and can set up more club tricks for themselves by playing three rounds of the suit. But as declarer has the queen, jack and ten between the two hands and can play these on different club tricks, the opponents can win only two of the first three club tricks and declarer must make one.

4

Exploratory Bidding

In the previous chapter opener always held a 5-card suit with every other suit having fewer cards, so it was obvious which suit to open. We now cover the position where opener has two suits of equal length (which should be bid first?), or where opener has a balanced hand (should opener start with 1NT or one of a suit?).

When you have two 5-card suits and enough strength to open we advise: start with the higher ranking first, planning to bid the lower ranking on the next round, unless you happen to hold the top and bottom suits (clubs and spades) in which case you should open 1♣.

This approach should make it easier to end in the right trump suit than starting with, say, the better quality suit. Suppose you held this hand as dealer:

> ♠ A 10 9 3 2
> ♡ A Q 5 4 3
> ◇ K 3
> ♣ 9

You have 13 HCP and 2 long-suit points (1 for each 5-card suit), a sound opening bid. You want to mention both hearts and spades in the auction, and wish to keep the bidding low as you do so to give most room for exploration. You might think 'Not only are the hearts the better suit, but they are also the lower one to bid, so I will begin by bidding 1♡.' The flaw in this idea arises on the next round when partner explores by bidding one of the other suits, say 2♣.

You pursue your plan of mentioning your second suit, 2♠, but spot two snags. First the bidding is actually higher up than if you had mentioned the spades first and then the hearts (e.g. 1♠ – 2♣ – 2♡). Also, partner knows that you have no suit longer than the first. When you mention the second suit he may correctly assess that your first suit has five cards in it, but cannot yet know that the second suit has more than four. With three cards in each he will prefer to settle in your first suit, rather than your second. If the auction began 1♡ – 2♣ – 2♠ responder would have to go to 3♡ to show preference for your first suit. By contrast, if the auction starts 1♠ – 2♣ – 2♡ he can return to 2♠ when preferring your first suit. That is a whole level lower, a big bonus.

This advantage arises whenever you have what is called 'touching' suits, i.e. adjacent in rank, spades and hearts, hearts and diamonds, or diamonds and clubs. You should open the higher, and then bid the lower, in order to end up lower down than if you bid them the other way about.

Now suppose you have the two black suits, clubs and spades, the lowest and the highest-ranking. If you open 1♠ and partner suggests one of the red suits as trumps (2♦ or 2♡) you would have to go to 3♣ to tell him about the clubs. By contrast if you start 1♣ he will be able to respond 1♦ or 1♡ and you can re-bid 1♠, mentioning both suits at a level two lower than the other auction. Hence the advice to open 1♣. However we recognise many players prefer to give emphasis to the major suit. They would choose to open 1♠ and risk saying goodbye to the club suit if the bidding gets too high to show the clubs.

When your suits are non-touching in rank (spades and diamonds, or hearts and clubs) you could conserve bidding space if you knew in which of the other two suits partner was going to respond. But you do not, and the bidding may get too high for you to mention both. If so it is better to have told partner about your major suit (♠ or ♡), where the game contract is 4♠ or 4♡, than about your minor suit (♦ or ♣) where the game is the tougher 5♦ or 5♣.

For example, suppose you hold spades and diamonds. If you open 1♠ and partner responds 2♣ you can happily show the diamonds, 2♦. But if the response was 2♡, you would have to go 3♦ to show the diamonds, and to explore at this level would need at least a trick more than a normal opening. (If you don't find a fit, you will end in 3NT needing at least 25 points. Partner's response at the two level promised at least 9, so you need at least 16 to justify exploring at the three level.) If you have fewer than 16 points, you have left yourself the option of rebidding 2♠, showing at least five spades and an opening close to minimum. (Remember, when a suit is bid for the second time the bid is a limit bid, not an exploring bid.)

When you hold precisely one 4-card suit your shape must be 4-3-3-3 and when you hold precisely two 4-card suits your shape must be 4-4-3-2. Both shapes are also acceptable in shape for an opening 1NT (showing a balanced hand), so should you choose 1NT or 1 of a suit?

The key factor in the choice is this. 1NT is a limit bid, and therefore it has a precise 3-point range, whereas the opening bid at the one level in a suit is an exploratory bid with a range of 12 to 19 points. If your point count lies within the correct range for 1NT we strongly advise opening 1NT, as it is a much more accurate description of your hand than one of a suit. However, if your point count is outside the range for 1NT then you must open with one of a suit (if you have two 4-card suits, we will look at which in a moment).

What 3-point range does the opening 1NT show? The Acol system advises that 1NT should show a minimum opening. If you are stronger than this you open one of a suit and bid no-trumps on the next round.

As you might open with as few as 12 points (though it is perfectly sensible to pass some 12 point hands), the official Acol range for the opening 1NT is 12-14. We have emphasised this is the range in Acol, because players who learn their bridge in the USA or France will be advised to open 1NT on hands that are a trick stronger than this, namely 15-17.

The argument about whether it is better to use the 12-14 *weak* no-trump (or 13-15 if you don't open on 12) or the *strong* no-trump (15-17 or 16-18) has been raging since Acol began. One method cannot be greatly inferior to the other, or over the years it would have died out. There are arguments for and against both methods. If you were to partner a player you had not met before, the strength of your opening 1NT is the matter you would discuss first. Both methods are perfectly acceptable, but the weak no-trump is part of Acol and is the most popular in Britain, so it is the method used in this book.

Thus, if your shape is 4-3-3-3 or 4-4-3-2 with a point range of 12-14, you should open 1NT. If you have the balanced shape but your point count is in the range 15-19 you must open one of a suit, and bid no-trumps on the next round.

With 15-16 you should make a minimum no-trump rebid (over a response at the one level, rebid 1NT, over a response at the two level rebid 2NT). With 19 rebid 3NT, as when partner responds you know the side has at least 25 points, maybe more, and all no-trump bids are limit bids. With 17-18 you will jump one level to show the extra values, i.e. over a response at the one level (which shows 6+ points) rebid 2NT, and over a response at two level (showing 9+ points) rebid 3NT. Example, with diamonds as your only suit in a *flat* (i.e. very balanced) hand:

$$\spadesuit \, x \, x \, x \quad \heartsuit \, x \, x \, x \quad \diamondsuit \, x \, x \, x \, x \quad \clubsuit \, x \, x \, x$$

with:

12-14 HCP	open 1NT.
15-16 HCP	open 1◇, and over 1♡ or 1♠ rebid 1NT, over 2♣ rebid 2NT.
17-18 HCP	open 1◇ and over 1♡ or 1♠ rebid 2NT, over 2♣ rebid 3NT.
19 HCP	open 1◇ and over any response rebid 3NT.

With 4-3-3-3 and 15-19 HCP you open one of your only 4-card suit. When you have two 4-card suits and 15-19 HCP you must choose which to bid first. Again, there is no universal opinion on this matter. We give firm advice but acknowledge that you may find bridge players doing something different. Our advice is this: with two 4-card suits open the higher, unless you have hearts and spades in which case you should open 1♡.

The reason for this advice is that you plan to bid no-trumps on the next round. It will often not matter missing a 'fit' in a minor suit (diamonds or clubs) where game is eleven tricks, whereas you do not wish to miss a fit in a major suit (hearts or spades) where game is ten tricks. So when you have one major, you show it at once. Where you have both you bid the lower ranking, hearts, as you are waiting to see if partner responds 1♠. If he does, raise with your 4-card support. If he does not respond in spades, make your re-bid no-trumps. When your two suits are both minors, our advice is to open 1◊, but again, you may find players who prefer 1♣. Examples, with two 4-card suits, first both majors:

♠ x x x x ♡ x x x x ◊ x x ♣ x x x

with: 12-14 HCP open 1NT
      15-16 HCP open 1♡; raise 1♠ to 2♠ or 3♠,
                      Pass a response of 1NT, over 2♣/2◊ rebid 2NT
      17-18 HCP open 1♡; raise 1♠ to 3♠ or 4♠, raise 1NT to 2NT,
                      over 2♣/2◊ rebid 3NT
      19 HCP   open 1♡; raise 1♠ to 4♠, raise 1NT to 3NT,
                      over 2♣/2◊ rebid 3NT

Now with one major and one minor:

♠ x x x x ♡ x x ◊ x x x x ♣ x x x

with: 12-14 HCP open 1NT
      15-16 HCP open 1♠; Pass a response of 1NT,
                      over 2♣/2♡ rebid 2NT
      17-18 HCP open 1♠; raise 1NT to 2NT, over 2♣/2♡ rebid 3NT
      19 HCP   open 1♠; raise 1NT to 3NT, over 2♣/2♡ rebid 3NT

♠ x x x ♡ x x x x ◊ x x ♣ x x x x

with: 12-14 HCP open 1NT
      15-16 HCP open 1♡; over 1♠ rebid 1NT, Pass a response of 1NT,
                      over 2◊ rebid 2NT
      17-18 HCP open 1♡; over 1♠ or 1NT rebid 2NT,
                      over 2◊ rebid 3NT
      19 HCP   open 1♡; raise 1NT to 3NT, over 1♠/2◊ rebid 3NT

Where responder shows the same minor as opener holds, opener has the option of rebidding in no-trumps, or of raising the minor. With a high card in his short suit, the doubleton, opener should normally prefer heading for the nine-trick game, 3NT.

It is possible to hold *three* 4-card suits (and a singleton in the fourth suit). You must not open 1NT with a singleton even if your point count is within your range for 1NT. We advise on which suit to open, but first a word of warning. 4-4-4-1 is the worst shape to pick up in bridge. You usually only get to tell your partner about two of your suits, and may miss a fit in the third. Also if you do bid two suits, your partner may rely on you having five cards in the first suit when actually you have only four. Fortunately this shape is a fairly rare one to pick up.

With a red-suit singleton (i.e. short diamond or short heart), we advise opening the suit below the singleton, intending, if partner responds in your short suit, to show the suit above the singleton.

With a black-suit singleton (i.e. short club or short spade) we advise opening with the middle of the three 'touching' 4-card suits. You hope partner will respond in the next suit up, which you then raise. If, as is more likely, he responds in your short suit, you then re-bid in the suit below the one you opened.

Assume you are the dealer with 13 HCP; here are the four shapes:

♠ x x x x   ♡ x x x x   ◇ x   ♣ x x x x

Easy. Open 1♣ and over 1◇ rebid 1♡, you can still find a spade fit. If partner responds 1♡ or 1♠, upgrade to 15 (you have a fit and a singleton) but raise only to 2♡/2♠. You need 16 or even 17 to jump to 3♡/3♠.

♠ x x x x   ♡ x   ◇ x x x x   ♣ x x x x

With non-touching suits open the suit below the singleton, 1◇. If partner responds 1♡, you rebid 1♠. If partner responds 1♠ or 2♣ you upgrade to 15 but make a minimum raise to 2♠ or 3♣.

♠ x   ♡ x x x x   ◇ x x x x   ♣ x x x x

With a singleton spade, open 1◇, the middle of three touching suits. If partner responds 1♡, up grade to 15 points, but raise only to 2♡. If partner responds 1♠ you must rebid 2♣ as 1NT would show 15-16.

♠ x x x x   ♡ x x x x   ◇ x x x x   ♣ x

With a singleton club, open 1♡, the middle of three touching suits. If partner responds 1♠, upgrade to 15, but raise only to 2♠. If partner responds 2♣ you must rebid 2◇, as 2NT would show 15-16.

We have now covered what to open on all possible shapes in which you have suits of equal length (if you ever see a 6-6 shape, treat it like 5-5).

We turn to the question of what partner should respond when he does not have the hand shapes covered in the previous chapter. These hands will be the ones on which responder wishes to explore by suggesting a new trump suit, rather than make a limit raise with 4-card support, or a limit response in no-trumps with a balanced hand.

Look at the following two hand-shapes mentioned in the section on MiniBridge:

West's longest suit is spades, East's longest suit is clubs, but the only suit in which the partnership has eight cards, and therefore an acceptable trump fit, is hearts. How can the partnership find this without the advantage of seeing partner's hand that you enjoy when choosing trumps in MiniBridge?

The answer is that the auction, with West opening, will go something like this:

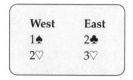

The first three bids are exploratory bids as it is the first mention of the suit. The bidder is not defining his hand strength to within one trick. Instead he is exploring for the trump suit and may have a wide range of strength. By contrast, when the heart fit is located and East raises to indicate this, East's raise, being the second time hearts have been mentioned, is a limit bid, defining his hand strength to within one trick. If East knows the partnership has enough points for game, he does not have to bid game whilst he is exploring, but must raise to 4♡ rather than 3♡ when the fit is found.

The opener's partner should respond with six points or more (opener may have 19 points and a fit in some suit as yet undiscovered, giving the partnership enough for game). The limit response ranges (when raising or showing a balanced hand) were 6-9, 10-12 and 13-15. By contrast, when exploring, responder will make the same response whatever of these strengths he has, giving priority to the need to keep the

bidding low whilst the two players are seeking the trump suit.
Example:

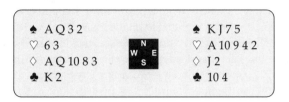

West with 15 HCP and 1 long-suit point opens 1◊, exploring. East with 9 HCP and 1 long-suit point responds only 1♡, exploring (6-15). West rebids 1♠, still exploring. East, locating the spade fit, intends to raise, which will be a limit bid. East upgrades by one point, maybe two for his short suits. Either way he is worth a raise to 3♠ (showing 10-12). West, hearing of the spade fit, could also upgrade for his short suits, but already has enough extra to go on to 4♠. The full auction has been:

West	East
1◊	1♡
1♠	3♠
4♠	Pass

This contract should make unless the cards lie very badly. You must lose a heart and a club. There are two finesse positions, the key one in diamonds that you must try as you have to establish your diamonds, and the one in clubs that you will leave as late as possible.

You expect to make four trump tricks by power, and maybe one with a ruff, at least four diamond tricks, and one heart. You have the king of clubs as a possible trick in reserve.

Now contrast the auction 1♡-1NT we had in the previous chapter, with the auction 1♡-1♠. They may look similar but in reality they are fundamentally different. The 1NT response is a limit bid showing 6-9 points whereas the 1♠ response is exploratory with a range of 6-15. (We reserve a jump bid in a new suit to show at least 16 points, and a guarantee that the side can easily make a game contract, and might start thinking about slam.)

All limit bids can be Passed. The 1NT response would be Passed whenever opener was happy with the denomination and knew the side did not have enough points for game. By contrast, when responder explores and can have up to 15 points, opener (in the range 12 to 19) must cater for the possibility that the side should reach game. Opener must make another bid so the auction does not finish prematurely at too low a level.

This agreement, that where a player opens, and his partner explores, the opener will bid again, is one of the most important in bidding. It is this that allowed responder, even when holding 15 points, to respond only 1♠ rather than anything higher. He knows he will get a further chance to show his strength on a later round of the auction, because opener has promised to bid again, and there cannot be three consecutive Passes.

The main purpose behind the exploratory response is to seek the best denomination for the final contract. The principal information conveyed is therefore about shape, the number of cards in each suit, the main determining factor in choice of trump suit. So the response of 1♠ to an opening of 1♡ says: 'Assume I have fewer than four cards in your suit and at least four cards in the suit I suggest as trumps. If I subsequently bid another suit, you may assume it has no more cards in it than the one I bid first. My strength range is 6-15 because with fewer than 6 I would have Passed the opening, and with more than 15 I would have jumped the bidding.'

Now suppose opener raises responder's bid one level, i.e. compare 1♡ – 1NT – 2NT with 1♡ – 1♠ – 2♠.

These look similar, but by now you should realise they are fundamentally different. Where East made the limit response of 1NT (6-9), opener could Pass. The raise to 2NT showed not only that West was accepting no-trumps but also that he had extra values, with a chance of 3NT (i.e. 17 or 18). With 19 he would raise 1NT to 3NT, knowing the side had at least 25 points and maybe more. With fewer than 17 he would have Passed 1NT knowing the side has at most 25 points, and maybe less. 2NT was an invitation for East to go on to 3NT if he held 8 or 9 points.

By contrast, when East explores by bidding a new suit, West, the opener, must not Pass. So now when he raises 1♠ to 2♠ he is saying: 'We have found the trump suit, but I am minimum for my opening.' If West held as many as 17 points (having upgraded for his short suits), he would jump to 3♠ to show both that the trump suit had been found, and that he had values at least a full trick better than a minimum opening. If West's point count was now 19-21, he would actually raise all the way to 4♠.

Here is an example:

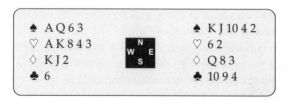

The Daily Telegraph Easy Guide to Acol Bridge

West has 17 HCP and 1 long-suit point and opens 1♡. East has 6 HCP and 1 long-suit point and responds 1♠. West, knowing of the spade fit, upgrades his hand by two points for the singleton club, making 20 in total, and raises the response to 4♠. The auction has been:

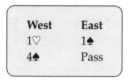

West	East
1♡	1♠
4♠	Pass

This contract should make in some comfort. East will clearly lose a trick in clubs and another trick to the ace of diamonds but he may well manage to make the other 11 tricks. You can easily see five spade tricks, two heart tricks, and two diamond tricks. The extra tricks will probably come from ruffing two of East's small clubs in the West hand. But to do this you will need to postpone drawing trumps as unless they break 2-2 you would leave yourself with not enough trumps in the West hand to trump the losing clubs.

In the previous example, East was able to suggest his suit as trumps without raising the level of the auction. But swap his spades and club holdings so East holds:

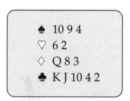

♠ 10 9 4
♡ 6 2
♢ Q 8 3
♣ K J 10 4 2

To show his club suit East would have to bid 2♣.There is a snag if East explores at a higher level with only a bare response of 6 or 7 points. The opener may have a minimum opening, and if the side has no fit, they will not have enough strength to make 2NT (where you need 22-24 points). So responder should only explore at the two level when he has at least 9 points, i.e. a trick better than the absolute minimum response. Responder with 6 to 8 points should even prefer to show a 4-card suit at the one level rather than over-reaching to the two level to show a 5-card suit.

East must respond with 6-points in case the side has game. So what, you may be thinking, does East respond if his suit or suits are lower ranking than the one opened, and he has only 6 to 8 points, such as on the hand shown above? The answer is that he must respond 1NT even if his hand is not particularly balanced. The response of 2NT or 3NT will always show a balanced hand, as responder had the alternative of exploring.

The 1NT response, however, may merely be the lesser of two evils, where the alternative was exploring at the two level with insufficient strength.

Where responder has a no-trump shape such as 4-3-3-3 or 4-4-3-2 is it better to mention one of the suits, or respond in no-trumps? If you can show a major suit at the one level you should do so, otherwise it is fine to respond in no-trumps. If opener does not raise the major-suit response, you can still end in no-trumps, but if you respond in no-trumps initially you may never find the major suit fit. For example:

♠ J 9 4
♡ K J 7 2
◇ J 8 3
♣ Q 10 4

If partner opens 1♣ or 1◇ you respond 1♡ (opener might have four hearts) but if he opens 1♠ you must say 1NT.

This consideration also affects the choice of response when you have 4-card support for opener's minor, but also have a major suit of your own. You should mention your major. If opener does not raise it you can always return to his initial suit, whereas if you raise the minor at once, you may miss a fit in the major where game is one trick fewer than in a minor. Example:

♠ J 9 4
♡ K J 7 2
◇ J 8
♣ Q 10 3 2

If partner opens 1◇ you respond 1♡ and then over 1♠ bid 1NT.
If partner opens 1♣ you also respond 1♡ but over 1♠ then go 2♣.

If responder has two suits of equal length to show at the one level which should he show first? The answer with two 4-card suits is 'the first available'. Example:

♠ Q J 9 3
♡ 9 8 4
◇ A K 6 2
♣ 10 4

If the opening is 1♡ respond 1♠, the first suit you can show.
But over 1♣ respond 1◇ as you can find a spade fit later.

With two 5-card suits, you must give priority to bidding a major suit, and take the chance to show the other if you get it. Example:

```
♠ A 10 6 3 2
♡ 9 3
◇ K 9 5 3 2
♣ 5
```

Respond 1♠ whatever the opening, you may have to say goodbye to the diamonds.

If you had 11 points you could respond 1♠ and have enough to show diamonds later.

Summary of Exploratory Bidding

- When opening the bidding with two 5-card suits, bid the higher ranking first. An exception arises when you have the two black suits (clubs and spades) where it is acceptable to open 1♣ and rebid 1♠.

- When opening the bidding with one 4-card suit, always open 1NT if you are in the range 12-14 HCP, otherwise, in the range 15-19 open your 4-card suits and rebid in no-trumps.

- When opening with two 4-card suits, open 1NT in the 12-14 range. In the range 15-19 open the higher ranking unless you have four hearts and four spades, in which case open 1♡ (intending to rebid in no-trumps, but raising spades if partner shows that suit).

- When opening with three 4-card suits that are non-touching (i.e. a red singleton), open the suit below the singleton, but with three touching suits (i.e. a black singleton) open the middle suit.

- A response in a new suit to an exploratory opening is itself exploratory with a very wide range of strength (6-15). Opener MUST rebid as the side may have enough for game. If opener has 4-card support for responder's suit he will raise, a limit bid. So a minimum raise by opener implies that he has a point count close to a minimum opening (fewer than 17 points certainly). If opener knows his side has enough for game, he should raise straight to game, or jump partway to game with extra values just short of the amount needed for game.

Exercises for Exploratory Bidding

With the various pairs of hands shown below predict the recommended bidding, first assuming West is the dealer, and then when East is the dealer:

Q1

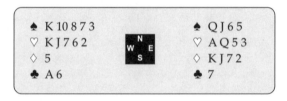

<table>
<tr><td>♠ K 10 8 7 3</td><td>♠ Q J 6 5</td></tr>
<tr><td>♡ K J 7 6 2</td><td>♡ A Q 5 3</td></tr>
<tr><td>◇ 5</td><td>◇ K J 7 2</td></tr>
<tr><td>♣ A 6</td><td>♣ 7</td></tr>
</table>

A1 West has 11 HCP + 2 long-suit points. When dealer, West should open 1♠, the higher of two touching 5-card suits. East has 13 HCP, upgrades to 15 points (two extra points for the singleton club as they have a spade fit) and raises 1♠ to 4♠. The auction is:

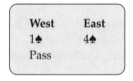

West	East
1♠	4♠
Pass	

When East is dealer he opens 1♡, the middle of three touching 4-card suits. West raises to 4♡ (the values might even suggest a raise to 5♡ as West upgrades to 16 points for the two short suits, but later you will learn of less risky ways to investigate chances that 6♡ is on). The auction is:

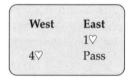

West	East
	1♡
4♡	Pass

So, depending on who opened, the side might reach 4♡ or 4♠. But don't worry, both make sensible game contracts, expecting to lose only a spade and a diamond. The opponents might get a ruff if they lead a singleton in the major suit that is not trumps, but that would be bad luck, and not fatal unless they got two ruffs (unlikely).

Q2

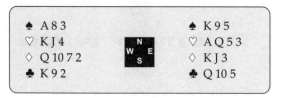

A2 Playing a weak no-trump if West is dealer he would open 1NT and East raise to 3NT. If East is dealer he must open 1♡ as the hand is too strong for 1NT, but then West will respond 3NT. On any lead (spades is best for the defence) declarer should play on diamonds to remove the defenders' ace whilst there are still winners in every other suit to regain the lead. Declarer can then make at least nine tricks with four hearts, three diamonds, and two spades, with hopefully a club to come later.

Q3

A3 With West as dealer the opening is 1♣. East might choose to respond 3NT, a perfectly acceptable game contract (with four club tricks, four heart tricks and the ace of spades), but could also choose to explore with 1◇. West then rebids 1♡, still exploring, and East raises to 4♡. This contract should make 10 or 11 tricks as declarer has the extra chance of a ruff or making the king of diamonds when North has the ace. If East is the dealer he opens 1♡ (too strong for 1NT, so open the major) and West raises to 4♡.

5

The Basics of Defence

On average, after the auction, a player becomes declarer on one quarter of the deals, dummy for a quarter of the deals, but a defender, trying to defeat the contract, on half the deals. Yet defence is generally considered the most difficult aspect of bridge. In bidding the system often determines the choice of bid, and in declarer play declarer can frequently see a guaranteed route to success. But in defence two players have to co-operate with information restricted to the bids made (mostly by opponents) and the cards played (with declarer usually dictating the line). With such restrictions two minds are not greater than one.

The first task of the defence is to choose the opening lead, often the determining factor in whether the contract succeeds or fails. But the defender has only the bidding and the sight of his 13 cards to help. After the lead has been made, down goes the dummy and the other players make their decisions having seen at least 27 cards.

When in doubt about what to do in defence, there are some useful tips.

First, leading from a sequence of high cards such as K Q J is much safer than leading an 'unsupported' ace, i.e. the ace without the king to back it up, a lead that many beginners are wrongly inclined to prefer. An ace will usually win a trick whether played at trick one or later when that suit is first led. If it is led at trick one declarer will contribute only small cards, whereas later the ace may well not only win the trick but also capture an opponent's king or queen, thereby reducing declarer's winners. Also when you lead from a sequence and find declarer has the ace, it is a trick declarer was always going to make, and having removed it, you now have created winners in the suit to make when your side next gains the lead.

When leading from a sequence such as K Q J x or Q J 10 x does it matter which card in the sequence is led? From your point of view they are equal in value, and if partner knew your cards, the answer would be no. But partner does not know your cards. If you led the queen from K Q and partner held the ace, fearing declarer held the king, partner might waste his ace on your queen unnecessarily. So defenders developed the practice of leading the *highest* card in a sequence. Partner will see you have led the king, and will not waste his ace.

As with agreements about what your bids mean, the Laws permit such carding agreements between defenders during the play, but the agreements must not be secret. If you have agreed with partner to lead '*top of a sequence*' in defence, as recommended in this book, then declarer is also entitled to know this. The deduction that when your lead is the queen, you do not hold the king (or you would have led it instead of the queen) is then equally available to both your partner and declarer.

The advice 'lead top of a sequence' applies to *honour* card leads (the top five cards in a suit: A, K, Q, J, 10) even when there is one card higher than the sequence, but not to cards below an honour. Holding K J 10 3 you should lead the jack and this would be called 'top of an *interior* sequence'. Similarly, from Q 10 9 3, you would lead the ten, but if you held Q 9 8 3 the nine and eight would be too low to be deemed a relevant sequence. We will define in a moment which card you should lead from such a holding.

Example: the opponents bid 1♠ – 4♠ – Pass.

From this hand:

```
♠ 6 3
♡ A 9 3 2
♢ Q J 10 5
♣ 9 5 2
```

The lead of the diamond queen would be much better than the lead of the heart ace.

Next tip: when leading against a no-trump contract it is usually right to start with the suit in which you have the most number of cards. If the auction is as uninformative as 1NT – 3NT – Pass, the only clue you have to declarer's weak spot is that the suit in which declarer has fewest cards is likely to be the one where you have most. If your longest suit is headed by a sequence of three cards in a row you should follow the first tip and lead top of that sequence. But if your long suit has only one high card then it is best to lead a low card. For example, suppose your holding in your longest suit was: A 9 6 5 3.

This suit would make a good lead against a no-trump contract and it would be wrong to lead the ace. It is better to lead a low card. Later, if your partner wins a trick, he can lead your suit again and then not only might your ace capture one of declarer's high cards, but also you have the opportunity to lead the suit a third time, quite possibly removing declarer's remaining cards in the suit. Your last two cards, though small, will now be winners, and you can cash them if you get the lead again later in the play.

Having decided not to lead the ace, does it matter which you lead of the smaller cards? From your point of view it will make no difference whether you lead the 3, 5 or 6. But you have a partner and if you agree

---

which of these cards you will lead partner is able to make some very useful deductions from the card you actually lead.

By far the most popular agreement about this matter both in Britain and, indeed, throughout the world, is that when leading a low card from your longest suit against a no-trump contract, you will lead the *fourth* card from the top of the suit. In the example A 9 6 5 3 the fourth card from the top *(fourth-highest)* is the 5, and that is the card you should lead. From the earlier example, Q 9 8 3, the fourth-highest is the 3 and this is the card you should lead.

To see the significance of this agreement for your partner, imagine you are sitting on the other side of the table, third to play after dummy. The auction has gone 1NT – 3NT – Pass, and your partner leads the two of spades. What can you deduce? He has led from his longest suit, he has chosen to lead a low card (so does not have a suit headed by three big cards in a row), and most important of all, if the two is his fourth-highest card, then he must have exactly four. (If he led the fourth-highest from a 5-card suit, he would have a card below the one led, and you know that is not the case because the two is the lowest card in the suit.) So you know partner has exactly four spades, you can see how many spades there are in dummy, and you know how many you have yourself. Hey presto! By subtracting this total from 13 you know at once how many spades declarer has without having seen his hand.

This is such an important deduction that it is worth another example. After the same simple auction 1NT – 3NT – Pass, your partner's opening lead is the three of spades, presumably from his longest suit. What else can you deduce? The answer depends on whether you can see the two of spades. Suppose you can see the 2 in dummy, or your own hand, or maybe when declarer plays a card to the first trick. Then the 3 was partner's lowest card in the suit, and if you have agreed to lead fourth-highest he must have exactly four. By contrast if the two of spades is not yet visible you know only that partner had four or five cards in the suit. You learn which when you see the 2. If partner later plays the 2, it will mean he originally held five cards in the suit. If declarer has the 2, the opening leader originally had four cards in the suit.

Such deductions, not easy for beginners, are the key to good defence. skillful bridge players keep an eye on even the smallest cards for, as you now see, the placing of a lowly 2 contains a vital clue to the unseen cards. It is not against the Laws to *false-card* (for example, by leading the fifth-highest rather the fourth), just as it is not against the Laws to bluff in the bidding. Bluff-bidding *('psyching')* is rarely used in bridge because of the dangers arising from misleading partner. However, in the play, false-carding is more common because a defender may judge the information from a true card will be more helpful to declarer than partner (remember your carding agreements are also available to the opponent). But general advice must be: for the opening lead, keep to your leading agreements. Knowing which card you lead from a particular holding is much more likely to be of help to partner than declarer.

If your sequence of cards at the top a suit is two in a row (for example: K Q 4 2) should you lead high or low? When the contract is a trump contract the first two rounds of a suit are much more important than the third when declarer may have no more cards in the suit and be able to trump. So you should lead high. The danger in leading low from K Q 4 2 is that declarer has both the jack and ace, and can trump the third round, leaving you with no tricks in the suit at all. By leading high you guarantee that you can win a second round of the suit. By contrast, if the contract was no-trumps, it would normally be right to lead a low card. Even if this gives declarer a cheap trick you still have the king and queen to win later tricks. If your suit was headed by a holding such as K Q 10 x, Q J 9 x, or J 10 8 x, this might be described as 'two-and-a-half in a row' because there are two high cards in sequence followed a gap of one card before the next in sequence). Best practice here is to lead high whether the contract is trumps or no-trumps. If you hold K Q 10 x you are hoping that where declarer has the ace and jack, the jack may be doubleton and your two high cards will *pin* the jack leaving the ten as master when the ace has gone.

When leading against a trump contract the tip about the early rounds of a side suit being crucial also influences the choice of lead from a holding such as the earlier example of A 9 6 5 3. To lead the ace is not particularly attractive, but it will normally be much less risky than leading a low card in the suit (the preferred choice when the contract has no trumps). Suppose in this side suit declarer had a singleton and the king in either hand, then *underleading* your ace would leave you with no trick in the suit at all, as declarer could trump it on the second round. So when choosing to lead against a suit contract from a suit headed by the ace you should lead the ace.

A lead that may work well against a trump contract is a singleton in a side suit. You are hoping your partner has a chance to play the suit a second time before declarer has drawn trumps. You can win the trick with a small trump by ruffing. This works best when partner has the ace of the suit you lead, or perhaps the ace of trumps, so that when declarer tries to draw trumps partner is able to win the trick and give you the ruff you wanted. Note the lead of a singleton is less attractive if your own trump holding was, for example, Q J 10, where you will make a trick by power without needing to ruff.

Frequently the opening leader will have no obvious good lead. To lead a trump is more often wrong than right. Declarer's plan is usually to draw trumps early, and the lead of a trump helps him with that task. But a trump lead can be best for the defence on a deal where declarer needs to obtain ruffs in dummy before drawing trumps.

Where partner has bid a suit that will often be the right suit to lead. Where only the opponents have bid, to lead a suit bid on your right (i.e. by declarer) is much more dangerous than leading a suit bid on your left (i.e. dummy). In the first case partner has to choose what to card to play in front of declarer's length and strength in the suit. In the other case, declarer has to choose what card to play from dummy's length and strength before your partner makes his choice, a much happier position for your side.

Leading from two or three small cards in an unbid suit is relatively neutral in the sense that it can turn out well or badly equally often. In Britain the normal card to lead from two small cards is the highest. From three small cards opinions differ about which is the best card to lead. We suggest you agree to lead *'top of nothing'*, i.e. the highest of the three, in order to help partner distinguish from the situation when you have chosen to lead low from a suit headed by one high card.

Enough on the opening lead. We turn now to play by the defender who is third to play. The main tip here is that if the first two cards played to the trick are small ones, it will be the third player's duty to make the declarer work to win the trick by playing a high card, even when the defender knows his card will be beaten.

For example, suppose the auction has gone 1NT – 3NT – Pass and partner leads the two of spades (fourth-highest of his longest suit).

Dummy goes down with three small cards and your holding in the suit is J 8 3:

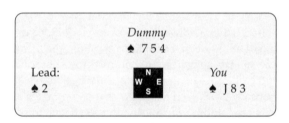

You might think 'partner cannot have A K Q in the suit as he would have led high, so I know my jack will be beaten by declarer, therefore I will keep the jack for later.' Right deduction, wrong conclusion! Suppose declarer has a holding such as A K 9. By withholding your jack you allow declarer to win a cheap trick with the nine, and he still makes his two big cards later, and three tricks in all. Had you played 'third-hand high' you would force declarer to use his ace or king, and partner would later prevent the nine taking a trick, holding declarer to two tricks in the suit.

Now suppose with the same lead of ♠ 2 from partner against 3NT, dummy's holding in the suit is J 5 4. What would you do, if:

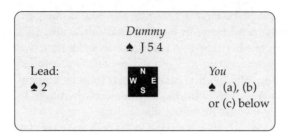

Dummy
♠ J 5 4

Lead:
♠ 2

You
♠ (a), (b)
or (c) below

(a) You held Q 9 6 and declarer called for the jack from dummy?
(b) You held Q 10 6 and declarer called for a small card from dummy?
(c) You held Q 9 6 and declarer called for a small card from dummy?

In (a) it would be right to play the queen to prevent declarer winning a cheap trick with the jack.

In (b) it would be correct to play the ten as that will be high enough to force out declarer's ace or king without wasting the queen.

But in (c) your decision is much more difficult. The nine would be best if partner held the ten as this would be good enough to force out declarer's ace or king, but the queen would be the winning play if partner held A K x 2 and declarer the 10. This shows how difficult defence can be.

Now suppose partner has led low, dummy has three small cards and you hold Q J x. You will follow the tip of third-hand high, but does it matter whether you play the jack or queen? From your point of view, no, as when you have adjacent cards they become equal in value to the holder. But you have a partner, and it may be helpful for him to know which card you play from 'equals'. If you play the jack and declarer wins with the ace, partner, holding the king, will deduce you have the queen as otherwise declarer would have won with the cheaper card. So the agreement developed that third hand, when playing high, would contribute the lowest card from a high sequence.

A consequence of this agreement then becomes that if you, in third seat, play the queen, partner knows you do not have the jack. Similarly if you play the king partner knows you do not have the queen.

The greater the strength of the declaring side, the more often they will win tricks and be leading to the next trick. To most tricks declarer or dummy leads and the defenders play second and fourth. The player in fourth seat for the most part has an easy task. He simply inspects the three cards already played. If an opponent is currently winning the trick he will beat their card as cheaply as possible, otherwise he contributes a small card. You may think this advice is obvious, and it will certainly be right most of the time. But there are very few 'rules' in bridge that are true in all circumstances. There are many exceptions to every rule. For example, it might be right to *overtake* (i.e. beat) your partner's winner because of the need for your hand to lead to the next trick rather than partner. It might be right to let declarer win the trick even when you could do so because you work out that is better for your side later in the play. And so on. The fact that each situation must be thought out for itself is part of the attraction of bridge. If you merely had to follow a fixed set of rules, bridge would be far less fascinating.

The defender who plays second to the trick has a much more difficult decision as to what card to play. If the first card played is a small one it will more often be right for the next player to play low as well. In the days of whist this tip was described as 'second-hand plays low'. In bridge there are many exceptions to this rule, but it starts as a good guide for beginners in situations such as this:

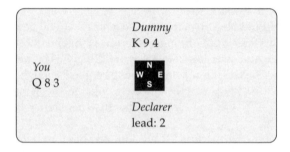

Declarer, whose holding in the suit is unknown, leads the 2. Which card should you play? Some beginners, misunderstanding the tip about third-hand high, think it is their duty to play the queen to force out declarer's king. Wrong! Partner is still there to save the day. If declarer is intending to play the nine from dummy partner may have the ten or jack to beat the nine. If declarer has both those cards then playing the queen is an error as it merely ensures it will not take a trick. Declarer is probably intending to play the king whatever you play, and therefore there is no point to playing the queen. That is the basis of the tip 'second-hand low'.

To show you life is not that easy here are a couple of exceptions. Look at this holding, very similar to the previous one, but where we have improved your holding from Q 8 3 to Q J 3:

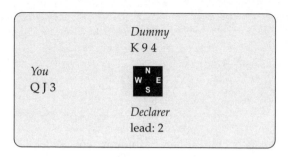

Dummy
K 9 4

You
Q J 3

Declarer
lead: 2

Again, declarer, whose holding in the suit is not known, leads the 2. Should you play high or low? The answer is that you probably do better to play high. The reason is that now if declarer has both the ten and ace he might be planning to insert the nine which, if you play low, would win the trick leaving you with no trick in the suit. Had you played high, forcing out the king, then declarer may later make the ace but you will control the third round of the suit.

Now suppose you are defending against a trump contract, and declarer leads a side suit where, next to play, you hold the ace and dummy has the king, i.e.

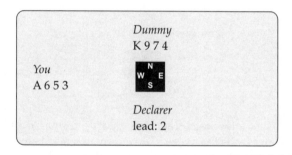

Dummy
K 9 7 4

You
A 6 5 3

Declarer
lead: 2

If declarer's holding is a singleton you may have to take your ace now or never. (If you play low, the king could win and declarer will be trumping the next round.) By contrast, if dummy's highest card was the queen, it would usually be safe to play low holding the ace, as either partner has the king to beat the queen, or declarer has it and you can beat his king later with your ace.

Now go the other side of the table and suppose this is what you see:

Dummy
Q 4 3

You
K 6 5

If declarer leads a low card from dummy, you will follow the tip of second-hand low and play small. By contrast, if declarer leads the queen it is normally right to put on the king even if you knew that declarer would beat this in turn with the ace. Whist players, referring to the five biggest cards in each suit, would advise 'cover an honour with an honour'. If you didn't declarer could win first the queen and then, on a later trick, the ace as well. Of course, if the dummy was to your left and you could see dummy held A J 10 9 then there would be no point in playing your king when the queen was led as that would leave no chance of a trick in the suit.

Change dummy slightly so the position is:

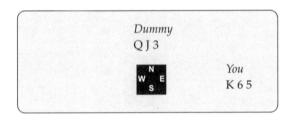

Dummy
Q J 3

You
K 6 5

If declarer leads a low card from dummy it is normal to play low. But what if declarer leads the queen? The queen and jack, being in the same hand, have become equal in value, so you have a choice whether you beat the first or second honour that is led. The best play is usually to beat the last of the equal cards to be led, i.e. don't play your king on the first honour led by dummy, but cover when he plays the last honour. One reason is that declarer might hold singleton ace and be forced to play it early anyway. Another, more complex, reason is that declarer might hold: A 9 8 x.

If you play the king the first time round, declarer can win the ace, and then prevent your partner's ten winning a trick by use of a finesse. Had you played low on the first honour led from dummy, your side would have the advantage when declarer next led the suit. If he led high you would cover and even though declarer would beat this with the ace, partner's ten would take the next trick. If declarer instead led low to the second round of the suit, you also play low and either you or partner must win a trick now or later.

To conclude, remember that the main objective in defence is to defeat the contract. So always keep track of how many tricks you need to do this. If you can see your way to that number of tricks, take it.

Summary of Basics of Defence

- Good leads: Top of a sequence; fourth-highest of longest suit *vs* no-trumps; singleton in a side suit *vs* a trump contract; partner's bid suit. Neutral leads: top of nothing, top of a doubleton *vs* a suit contract. Dangerous leads: from an unsupported honour; up to declarer's bid suit.

- Third hand play: play high after first two hands play low. With a high sequence, play the lowest of the sequence.

- Second-hand play: play low when first hand leads low, unless you have a high sequence; cover an honour with an honour; cover the last honour led.

- Keep track of the number the number of tricks needed to beat the contract, and take them when possible.

Exercises for Basics of Defence

Q1 The auction goes 1NT – 3NT – Pass and you are on lead with a 5-card suit. What card would you lead from that suit holding:
(a) K Q J 3 2; (b) K Q 10 3 2; (c) K J 10 3 2; (d) K 10 9 3 2 (e) K 9 8 3 2 ?

A1 (a) The king (top of a sequence); (b) still the king as K Q 10 counts as a sequence; (c) The jack (top of an interior sequence); (d) The ten (still top of an interior sequence); (e) The 3 (fourth-highest, as the 9 8 do not count as a high sequence).

Q2 What card would you lead from this hand:

```
♠ 3
♡ 9 8 4
◇ K 9 8 5 3 2
♣ K Q J
```

if the auction has gone, starting on your right:
(a) 1♠ – 4♠ – Pass; (b) 1♡ – 4♡ – Pass (c) 1NT – 3NT – Pass?

A2 (a) The king of clubs. Even if declarer has the ace you set up two winners for when your side next gains the lead.
(b) The three of spades. A singleton is a good lead against a trump contract. You hope partner can return the suit for you to obtain a ruff before declarer draws trumps.
(c) The five of diamonds. Against no-trumps lead fourth-highest of your longest suit, not from a good but short sequence.

♠ ♡ ◇ ♣

Q3 What is your lead from this hand:

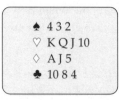

```
♠ 4 3 2
♡ K Q J 10
◇ A J 5
♣ 10 8 4
```

if the auction has gone, starting on your right, with only the opponents bidding: 1♠ – 2♡ – 2♠ – 3♠ – 4♠ – Pass?

A3 You would normally lead an automatic king of hearts, but here the opponents' auction 1♠ – 2♡ – 2♠ – 3♠ – 4♠ – Pass has been very informative. An expert player would decide that dummy has five hearts (with only four hearts he would either bid no-trumps with a flat hand, raise spades with four, or show a lower 4-card suit if he had one), and three spades (dummy raised when declarer showed five cards in spades). Therefore dummy has at most five cards in the minors, and must be short (at most two cards) in one of them. Furthermore dummy has about 10 or 11 points to invite game when opener showed a minimum range opening by the limit rebid of 2♠, and declarer must have about 14 points to accept the invitation. Having made all those deductions a trump lead stands out as the lead to prevent declarer ruffing a minor suit loser in dummy. The full hand should be something like this:

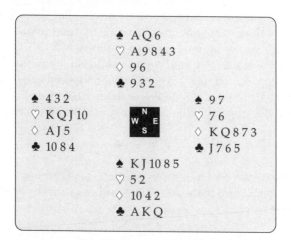

Declarer has nine obvious winners (five spades, one heart and three clubs) and three clear losers (two diamonds and a heart). On any lead but a trump he can arrange to ruff the third diamond in dummy for his tenth trick. The play would be: win the non-trump lead, play a diamond, win any switch by the defence and lead a second diamond, win any lead by the defence in the South hand and lead a third diamond, trumping in dummy, now draw trumps when you can and claim ten tricks.

On a trump lead declarer might decide his chance of ruffing a diamond has gone (the defence gain the lead twice in diamonds to lead a second trump, and then a third), preventing the diamond ruff.

If so declarer might switch to an alternative plan of setting up dummy's hearts, but West's good hearts prevent this. After the second trump lead by the defence dummy has insufficient entries to set up the hearts.

If you solved that lead problem you are, or are going to be, a very good bridge player. The point of the question was to show that an amazing number of clues may be there, to tell you when the 'normal' play is not the winning one.

Q4 The auction goes 1NT – 3NT – Pass and your partner, who is on lead, starts with the five of clubs. Dummy's club holding is: Q 10 7 6 and you hold, third to play K 8 2. What card do you play when declarer plays low from dummy?

A4 Did you think, third-hand high and play the king? Correct up to a point, but you failed to use the knowledge that partner has led the fourth-highest card in the suit led. Check it out and you find there are only three cards missing above the five and partner must have them all, namely his holding must be precisely A J 9 5. Declarer, who must have at least two cards in the suit to bid no-trumps, has the 4-3 doubleton. So your eight is good enough to win the first trick! If you play the eight your side will win three tricks in the suit. Had you played the king your side would only win two tricks in the suit.

Q5 The contract is 4♠. Dummy, to your left, has K 9 3 in clubs. Declarer leads a small card in the suit. What card would you play if you held:
(a) J 8 4   (b) J 10 4

A5. (a) The 4, second-hand low. To play the jack would be a clear error and may cost a trick when declarer has something like Q 10 x as your jack can no longer come into play.
(b) It is correct now to play the jack or ten just in case declarer was planning to put in the nine.

Q6 The auction went 1♠ – 4♠ – Pass. Partner, who is on lead, starts with the ace of clubs. This is what you see:

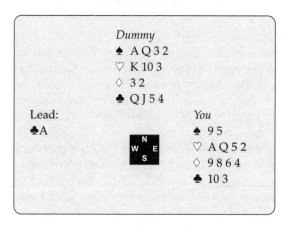

Dummy
♠ A Q 3 2
♡ K 10 3
◊ 3 2
♣ Q J 5 4

Lead:
♣ A

You
♠ 9 5
♡ A Q 5 2
◊ 9 8 6 4
♣ 10 3

Partner, bless him, continues with the king of clubs and a third one, which you trump, declarer following suit all the time. What do you play next?

A6 Your side has three tricks in the bag and you must now cash the ace of hearts to defeat the contract even though that sets up dummy's king. If declarer had a singleton heart it would disappear on dummy's winning club unless you make your ace of hearts now. Declarer might well hold a hand such as the one below.

♠ K J 10 x x
♡ x
◊ A K Q x
♣ x x x

6
Scoring

It may seem strange to get this far without detailed scoring, but beginners can enjoy bridge knowing simply that the more ambitious the contract the higher the reward if it makes, but that declarer loses points if the contract fails. The detail of bridge scoring can seem daunting. It is much easier to absorb once a player is familiar with various contracts, and how they can succeed or fail. Bridge scoring, roughly speaking, makes it attractive to bid a higher-bonus contract if declarer has a better-than-even-money chance of making the higher contract. But it can also be worthwhile to bid a contract that fails if the points you lose are fewer than the points you would have lost had you let the other side bid and make their contract. Bridge scoring also aims where possible to balance risk with reward.

The top-scoring bonus goes to the grand slam (a contract to make all 13 tricks). The next step down in bonus is the small slam (a contract to make 12 tricks), then the game contracts (5◇, 5♣, 4♠, 4♡ and 3NT) and finally the part-scores (those contracts worth less than a game).

Declarer can also increase his score by making overtricks (tricks in excess of the contract). Two calls, double and redouble, can change the scoring of a contract without affecting the contract itself.

We cover scoring both of Rubber Bridge, where one table is in play, and Duplicate Bridge, where more than one table is in play and the same deals are played at different tables. To start with we concentrate on Rubber Bridge but then mention the differences when playing duplicate.

Rubber bridge can be played for money but does not have to be. Poker can seem meaningless without money, but bridge can be enjoyed with no more than honour at stake. If you do choose to play for money the stake is usually described as so much per hundred points. This might vary between a penny-a-hundred (at this stake even a beginner is unlikely to win or lose more than a pound in an evening) up to stakes at a few London clubs where thousands of pounds change hands during an evening. When adding up at the end of a rubber of bridge, one loser pays one member of the winning side, and the other member of the losing side pays the other winner. You don't have to pay both.

A rubber of bridge is a contest lasting best-of-three games. The side that wins 2 games to 1 earns a reward of 500 points at the end of the rubber. The other possible outcome in games is 2-0 (you cannot win 3-0 as, once you are 2-0 ahead, the rubber ends) and the bonus for this is 700. There are many other ways to win or lose points. It is even possible for the side that finished ahead in games to end up the overall loser in the rubber because of the contracts they bid that failed, or perhaps a slam made by the opponents. In duplicate bridge each deal represents a separate battle, there is no such thing as a rubber, and bonuses for game are given on the deal where the game was bid and made.

The definition of a game is 'the value of contracts bid and made is worth 100 points or more'. At rubber bridge the value of contracts bid and made can be carried forward from one deal to the next until the 100 is achieved, perhaps over several part-score deals. At duplicate bridge the game must be bid on one deal.

The value of the contracts is:

For clubs and diamonds (the minor suits) 20 points per trick named
For hearts and spades (the major suits) 30 points per trick named
For no-trumps 40 points for the first trick named and 30 thereafter.

By 'trick named' we mean this: to make a contract of $2\heartsuit$ declarer must make eight tricks as the contract specifies how many tricks more than six ('the book') declarer must win. The value of the contract $2\heartsuit$ is $2 \times 30 = 60$, i.e. you only score the tricks made in excess of the book. The value of the contract $3\diamondsuit$ is 3×20, i.e. the same 60 even though declarer must win nine tricks to succeed.

You can now see why the game contracts are $5\clubsuit$ and $5\diamondsuit$ ($5 \times 20 = 100$), $4\spadesuit$ and $4\heartsuit$ ($4 \times 30 = 120$ whereas 3×30 is only 90 and not worth game), and 3NT ($40 + 30 + 30 = 100$). When the contract is no-trumps it is that crucial extra 10 points for the first trick named that brings the score for 3NT up to exactly the 100 points needed to make game in one deal.

The value of any overtricks (tricks made in excess of the contract) is:

For clubs and diamonds   20 points per overtrick
For hearts, spades, and no-trumps   30 points per overtrick

Overtricks are irrelevant in terms of achieving the bonus for a contract. It is only tricks both bid for AND made that count towards achieving the game bonus. So at rubber bridge where the value of contracts bid and made can be carried forward from deal to deal it is necessary to distinguish this value from overtricks made, and penalties received when the other side fails. The players therefore keep track of the score on a score-card that looks like Fig. 1 (overleaf):

The two columns marked We and They could equally well be thought of as Plus and Minus columns. Points your side wins from the opponents are recorded in the left-hand column, and points your side loses to the opponents are recorded in the right-hand column. At the end of the rubber each column is added up, and the difference between the two determines the winner and the size of the win.

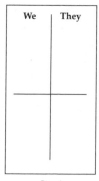

Fig. 1

The value of contracts bid and made are recorded BELOW THE LINE (so it is easy to spot when a side has made a game by seeing that these points add to hundred points or more). All other scores and bonuses are recorded above the horizontal line.

As an exercise, on a piece of paper, make out a rough score-card with the two columns headed We and They and the horizontal line two-thirds of the way down. Then keep track of the imaginary rubber of bridge described below in which 'We' means your side, and 'They' are your opponents. Remember the value of contracts bid and made go below the line, the value of overtricks goes above the line. You write the score starting by the point where the horizontal line and the vertical line cross and for later scores work outwards from that point. Let's score a rubber together.

On the first deal 'WE' bid 3◇ and make 10 tricks. Your score-card should look like Fig. 2.

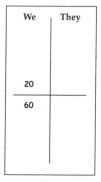

Fig. 2

When scoring the first thing to do is work out whether the contract succeeded or failed, because the scoring of failed contracts is completely different from that of successful ones. If the contract succeeded, put its value below the line in the column corresponding to declarer's plus points. Then work out if there were any overtricks and record the value of those above the line in the same column. On the first deal the contract of 3◇ succeeded and was worth 3 x 20 = 60. Declarer had to make nine tricks to make 3◇ but actually made 10 tricks so there was one overtrick worth 20 points recorded above the line.

On the second deal of the rubber THEY bid 2NT and make nine tricks. Record the score. Your score-card should now look like Fig. 3.

The contract of 2NT succeeded and its value is 40+30 = 70. This goes below the line in the THEY column as the opponents made it. The contract was to make eight tricks (two more than the book of six), but declarer achieved nine so he made one over-trick. This is worth 30 points (note the extra 10 for no-trumps arises only once, in the value of the contract made, and not in the overtricks as well).

We	They
20	30
60	70

Fig. 3

On the third deal of the rubber WE bid 2♡ and make 10 tricks. Record the score. Working outwards from the cross-point the value of the contract made goes below the score for the first contract WE made, and the value of the overtricks made goes above the previously recorded bonuses above the line. You should have spotted something else has happened. WE now have a total of 120 points below the line meaning our side has achieved game, indeed has won the first game of the rubber. To indicate the game is over draw a new horizontal line across both columns underneath the scores already recorded there. Your score-card now looks like Fig 4.

We	They
60	
20	30
60	70
60	

Fig. 4

Note: all the points scored so far will still count for either side at the end of the rubber, but as far as the second game, just about to start, is concerned, they are now *above the line*. Look at the 70 points THEY achieved towards the first game when THEY bid and made 2NT. THEY will still count that 70 points at the end of the rubber, but it cannot be carried forward to help them win the second game. The second game starts level between the two sides, with nothing below the new line for either .

On the fourth deal of the rubber WE bid 4♠ and make 10 tricks. Record the score. The contract of 4♠ requires 10 tricks to be made, and WE just made it. The value of the contract is 4 x 30 and the 120 is recorded below the line in our column. WE have just won the second game all in one go, so you should draw a new horizontal line underneath the 120 across both columns. But something else has happened. WE have won two games and therefore the rubber. As WE won the rubber 2-0 in games WE record a bonus of 700 points above the line. Now add up both columns. Your score-card should look like Fig. 5.

We	They
700	
60	
20	30
60	70
60	
120	
1020	100

Fig. 5

So WE have 1020 in our plus column and 100 in

the minus column (the THEY column). WE have won the rubber by 920 points. If we agreed a stake of a penny-a-hundred this is rounded to the nearest hundred. One of us claims ninepence from one of the losers whilst our partner receives ninepence from the other member of the losing side. At the end of each rubber players sitting out must be given a chance to come into the game, and, unless you have agreed to keep the same partners throughout a session, it would be normal to change partners.

Had the difference been 950 points would you have rounded up or down? The Laws of Bridge don't deal with money matters, believing such things are for private agreement between the players. Curiously rounding practice differs between the USA and Britain, and the practice corresponds to the national character. Can you guess which rounds up and which down? Americans have a philosophy of positive thought. They assume they will win more often than they lose and round up. The British (more in the past than now) traditionally sympathise with the poor losers so round down.

In that first rubber all the contracts succeeded. In real life many fail and the scoring of failed contracts is completely different from the scoring of successful ones. If a contract fails the value of the contract becomes irrelevant. The key thing is by how many tricks did it fail (the undertricks). The penalty for failing by one trick in the lowly contract of 1♣ is exactly the same as the penalty for failing by one trick in 7NT. The normal penalty is 50 points per undertrick to be recorded above the line in the defenders' column. So if WE failed by one trick put 50 above the line in the THEY column. There is another factor in deciding penalties that can be introduced by recounting the story of the birth of modern contract bridge on the 31st October and 1st November 1925.

Contract Bridge was preceded by Auction Bridge. When one side dropped out of the auction initially there was no encouragement in the scoring for the other side to continue bidding. In 1912 a British player, Hugh Clayton, experimented with bonuses for game and slam that would only be scored if both bid and made, and came up with the name 'contract'. At the end of the First World War some French players had the same idea and called their version Plafond (bidding to the 'ceiling'). But it was the American millionaire Harold Vanderbilt on the cruise ship S.S. Finland who put together a coherent set of bonuses and penalties that quickly led to contract sweeping aside auction.

Vanderbilt realised a side with a game already in the bag bid more ambitiously because the reward for winning the second game was so enticing. He wanted to balance risk and reward, and decided the penalties for failing when you already had a game should be doubled to 100 points per undertrick. The four men at the bridge table wanted a word to describe the situation when the penalty for failure would be twice as great. A woman watching, whose name is not known, came up with the word 'vulnerable'. The men liked that and then wanted a word to cover the situation where a side had not yet bid a game and so the penalties were less. I guess it was the men who thought and thought and came up with 'non-vulnerable', the ugliest word in bridge, but still with us today.

Now score a second rubber of bridge. Make out a fresh score-card with the two columns headed WE and THEY, and the horizontal line two-thirds of the way down.

On the first deal WE bid 4♡ and make nine tricks. Record the score.

4♡ is a contract to make ten tricks and WE made nine, so the contract failed and the penalty of 50 points is recorded above the line in the THEY column. Your score-card should look like Fig. 6.

On the next deal WE bid 3NT and make 10 tricks. Record the score. As the game contract succeeded your score-card should look like Fig 7.

On the next deal THEY bid 5♣ and make nine tricks. Record the score. The contract was to make 11 tricks, THEY made nine tricks. THEY have not scored a game yet and are non-vulnerable so the penalty is 2 x 50 and the 100 goes above the line for WE. The score-card looks like Fig. 8.

On the fourth deal of the rubber WE bid 4◊ and make eight tricks. Record the score. The contract was to make ten tricks and WE failed by two. Also WE are vulnerable, having already scored a game, so the penalty is 2 x 100 and the score of 200 goes above the line in the THEY column. The score-card looks like Fig. 9.

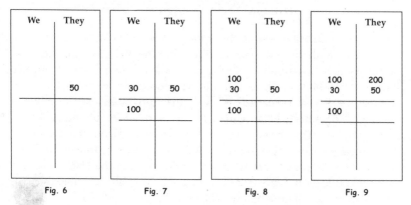

Fig. 6   Fig. 7   Fig. 8   Fig. 9

On the next deal WE bid 4♡ and make 10 tricks. Complete the score.

The game contract, worth 4 x 30 = 120 points succeeded and is recorded below the line in the WE column. We have made a game, so there is new horizontal line, and the rubber is over with WE having a bonus of 700 points above the line. The two columns are totalled, giving a score-card that looks like Fig. 10.

WE have 1050 in our plus column and 250 in the minus column so WE win the rubber by 800 points. At a penny-a-hundred each member of the winning side is eightpence richer.

We	They
700	
100	200
30	50
100	
120	
1050	250

Fig. 10

That completes the bulk of scoring but there is more to mention. The slam bonuses are recorded in the Table below. You score these bonuses if you both bid and make a slam. The bonuses are in addition to any reward for having made the game.

Table of Slam Bonuses

	Non-vulnerable	Vulnerable
Small Slam	500	750
Grand Slam	1000	1500

Note that if you fail in a slam the penalty of 50 or 100 may seem tiny by comparison with the bonuses for success, but the real loss is that had you been less ambitious you could have scored up game, and if already vulnerable, rubber. So there is a missed opportunity of scoring up, say between 600 and 850 points. This is why the vulnerable small slam bonus has to be 750 points to balance that loss. Similarly, if you bid a grand slam and fail by one trick the penalty is still only 50 or 100, but the real loss is the missed opportunity of scoring up the small slam, game and rubber. Together these bonuses are worth a little more than the 1500 bonus for the vulnerable grand slam and you need to be measurably more than 50-50 sure of success before bidding the grand.

We have briefly mentioned the calls of double and redouble that change the scoring of a contract without changing the contract and must now cover them in more detail. But first think about the tactic called *sacrificing*. Suppose one side is vulnerable and bids a game that will succeed. That side would score up at least 800 points (the value of the contract and the rubber bonus) and the other side score minus 800. The opponents, with a penalty for failing in their own contract of only 50 points per undertrick, would realise that it pays to bid on with a contract of their own, even when everyone knows it has no chance of success and may fail by several tricks. Sacrificing is a perfectly legitimate tactic but it would pay much too often but for the call of double that makes it less attractive.

Either member of a side may 'double' a contract bid by an opponent. If this doubled contract becomes the final contract (and three consecutive Passes are still required to finish the auction) then the penalty for failure is doubled if the contract fails by one trick. If the contract fails by two or more tricks the penalty is more than doubled. The Laws have progressively increased the penalty for doubled contracts in order to discourage sacrificing. This book is written as the 1993 Laws of Rubber Bridge and the 1997 Laws of Duplicate Bridge are in force. The penalties are the same in both, and are shown in the next Table.

Of course, if the only effect of doubling was to increase penalties, all contracts would be doubled, so to balance that, the value of the contract is also doubled if it succeeds. (There is a further reward for the doubled side if they succeed of 50 points called '50 for the insult' of having been doubled and the value of any overtricks are substantially increased. Slam bonuses are unchanged.) This makes a difference that is very significant for contracts such as 2♡ up to 4◇. The value of 2♡ as a contract is 60 points. If doubled and made it is worth 120 points, enough for game. Declarer has been doubled 'into game'. He still only has to make eight tricks to succeed but his reward will be much greater. So if you double an opponent into game you must be very confident you are going to defeat the contract.

Looking at the table below you can see that if a non-vulnerable side sacrifices against a vulnerable, making game, it remains profitable if the sacrifice fails by three tricks but, thanks to the double, not if it fails by four tricks. Without the double the sacrificing side could afford to bid a contract that made no tricks at all!

Table of Scores for Failing Contracts

Undertricks	Undoubled		Doubled	
	Non-vul	Vul	Non-vul	Vul
1 down	50	100	100	200
2 down	100	200	300	500
3 down	150	300	500	800
4 down	200	400	800	1100
Thereafter, each extra undertrick	50	100	300	300

Table of Scores for Successful Doubled Contracts

	Non-vulnerable	Vulnerable
Contract Value	Double normal	Double normal
Overtricks, each	100	200
Bonus	50 for the insult	50 for the insult

Note that when a contract is doubled the next three players all have a chance to remove to a higher contract which is then undoubled until one of the opponents chooses to double it. Here is an example:

West	North	East	South
1♡	1♠	2♣	Pass
2♡	Pass	3♣	Dbl
Pass	Pass	3♡	Pass
Pass	Dbl	All Pass	

West, as dealer, opened 1♡, North overcalled 1♠, and East responded 2♣. West then rebid 2♡ and East, not happy with hearts, tried clubs again. South, who also had good clubs, doubled as he was confident East could not make 3♣. Because of the double the next three players all have a chance to remove and East decided to do so, as he came to the conclusion hearts might prove a safer spot. South was not able to double this, but North with some values in hearts, aware that South knew the opponents could not make 3♣, doubled 3♡, confident West will not make that contract. This double is followed by three consecutive Passes so the auction ends. The final contract is 3♡ doubled with West as declarer.

Whenever a contract is doubled, either member of the doubled side may redouble, further increasing both the value for making the contract and the penalties for failing. It is a rare call as it implies the redoubling side reckons the doubling side have erred. Penalties for failing in a redoubled contract are exactly twice those for a doubled contract. If the contract succeeds the value of the contract is redoubled (e.g. 1♡ redoubled is worth 30 x 2 x 2 = 120, and would bring a game reward if it made). The 50 'for insult' becomes 100, and the overtricks are also worth twice as much as when doubled.

To complete rubber bridge scoring we mention some 'fun' bonuses abandoned long ago for Duplicate, but somewhat irrationally clung to by the Laws for Rubber Bridge. If one player holds four of the five honours (A, K, Q, J, 10) in the trump suit his side gets a bonus of 100 points. If one player holds all five trump honours, or all four aces in a no-trump contract his side is given a bonus of 150 points. A defender is permitted to claim this 'honour bonus', but, to avoid giving information to partner, must not do so until play is ended. By this time the cards have been thrown in the middle of the table, and the other players may doubt the claim!

Now we come to the scoring of duplicate bridge, much simpler than rubber bridge scoring. Each deal is a separate contest in itself so there is no carry-forward from one deal to another. This is essential because pairs will not necessarily play the deals in the same order, but the conditions must be identical for all who play a particular deal. So there is no 'above or below the line'. For successful contracts the contract value and bonuses are all added together and recorded as one score. For failing contracts the penalty is identical to rubber bridge and recorded in the defenders' column. The vulnerability is recorded on the board for all to see (usually a red dot against your name if your side is vulnerable and a white or green dot if you are not).

The bonus for a successful slam at duplicate is the same as for rubber bridge. For making games and part-scores the bonus must be given at once on each deal and not at the end of the rubber. These are:

Duplicate Bonus for Contracts Made

	Non-vulnerable	Vulnerable
Part-score	50	50
Game	300	500

The Laws, which are worldwide, actually specify the dealer and vulnerability for each numbered deal. For example, on Board 1 neither side is vulnerable and the dealer is North; on board 2 North-South are vulnerable and the dealer is East and so on. This means it is possible to play the same deals throughout the world and fairly compare scores between players not only in different clubs, but in different continents. Comparison of scores when many tables, even thousands, have played the same deals, would be arduous, but it is done by the tournament organiser using a computer, and perhaps the internet. The players have only the responsibility of entering the score for their table accurately.

Each deal has its own score-slip attached to the board that travels with the board. This travelling score-slip is folded so new players of the deal cannot see what others did before them on the deal. When play is complete North records the score achieved at his table on the score-slip that looks like this:

N/S Pair	E/W Pair	Contract	By	Tricks Made	N/S+	E/W+	N/S MPs	E/W MPs
Travelling Score Sheet Board 5								
1								
2								
3								
4	8	3NT	N	11	660			
5								
6								
7								
8								
9								
10								
11								
12								

The number of the board to which the score-slip belongs is recorded at the top right-hand corner. Each pair in the tournament has a number. North always does the scoring. If North's pair number is 4 he looks for his row on the score-slip, indicated by the left-hand column. In the adjacent column he writes the pair number of the opponent, then the final contract and result, which player was declarer, and finally the score. The score goes in the left-hand score column (the equivalent of the WE column in rubber bridge) if North-South achieved a plus score, and in the right-hand column (the equivalent of the THEY column for rubber bridge) if North-South had a minus score. North then folds the slip so the results cannot be seen by the next group to play the deal, and returns the slip to the board.

(In case you are wondering, the last two columns on the right are reserved for the tournament scorer, who, for each pair, compares their score with every other pair holding the same cards, awarding "Match-points" for each result.)

Summary for Scoring

- Scoring balances risk with reward. Roughly speaking, it rewards contracts with a higher bonus enough to make them worth bidding when you have a better than even money chance of success. A game means a contract with a value of 100 or more (if bid on one deal: 3NT, 4♡, 4♠, 5♣, or 5♢), a small slam is any contract of 12 tricks, and a grand slam any contract to make all 13 tricks.

- In rubber bridge the value of contracts bid and made go below the line and may be accumulated from one hand to the next until a game is made. All other bonuses and penalties go above the line. In duplicate bridge there is only one score per deal. For successful contracts this is the sum of the contract value, any overtricks, and the contract bonus.

- The scoring of failed contracts is completely different but is identical for rubber and duplicate bridge. A side that already has a game is vulnerable (at duplicate the vulnerability is shown artificially on the board) and the basic penalty per undertrick is 100 instead of 50. If a contract is doubled or redoubled the contract remains unchanged but both the penalty for failure and the reward for success is increased. The ability to double an opponent's contract makes sacrificing by them a less attractive option.

- No exercises are given for this chapter as you should have been practising as you went along.

7

The Opening One No-trump and Responses

No-trump bids are limit bids, namely the strength of the hand is known to within a 3-point range. The opening 1NT shows a hand, balanced in shape, and in the Acol system, a minimum in terms of opening strength, i.e. 12-14 points. All hands 4-3-3-3 in shape (and nearly all hands of 4-4-3-2 in shape) should be opened 1NT provided the point count is within the agreed range. Some hands of 5-3-3-2 in shape (where the 5-card suit is a minor) and the right point count should open 1NT (the alternative is to open and then repeat the minor). If the 5-card suit is a major suit, where game is only one trick more than in no-trumps, then preference should be given to opening the major and rebidding it at the lowest level to show at least five cards in a minimum-strength opening hand.

When your partner has opened 1NT you know his strength to within one trick and the first question to ask yourself is 'Is there a game on?' Your response will depend on whether the answer to this question is No, Yes or Maybe. The partnership strength needed to make 3NT is 25 points. So if responder has 10 points or less the answer will be 'No', with 11 or 12 points it will be 'maybe,' and with 13 or more it will be 'Yes.' (Two opening bids facing each other should together be enough to make a game contract.) If you have agreed a different range of opening no-trump (i.e. not 12-14) the responding strengths needed for a particular action would be adjusted but the same scheme of responses would be used.

Suppose first responder has a balanced hand and is happy with no-trumps as the denomination for the final contract. Then his course of action if he knows there is no game is to Pass the opening 1NT. If responder knows there is a game (i.e. with 13 or more points) he bids 3NT. With the 'Maybe' strength of 11 or 12 points, responder raises 1NT to 2NT. In effect responder is sitting on the fence between Passing and raising to Game. He is said to be 'inviting' game. Responder is in doubt because he does not know where in the range 12-14 opener's strength lies. So opener rejects the invitation by Passing the 2NT response when his strength is at the bottom end of the range, and accepts by going on to 3NT when he is at the top end of the range. (If spot in the middle rely on other factors such as your tens and nines, or the relative strength of the opposing pairs, to make up your mind.)

Note that responder with the strength to hope for eight tricks but not enough to make nine should Pass 1NT because if he raises to 2NT opener will go on to 3NT whenever opener is at the top end of his range. So responder can Pass with up to 10 points. Contrast that with the response to an opening One of a suit. The upper limit for an exploratory opening bid at the one level is 19 points so responder bids with 6 or more to allow for the possibility that the side has 25 points between them. With the weak opening no-trump opener has at most 14 points so there is no need for a response even with 10 points.

Partner opens 1NT, showing 12-14 points and a balanced hand. Holding the following hands, you would bid:

(a)	(b)	(c)
♠ J 8 6	♠ K 8 6	♠ K 8 6
♡ K 7 4	♡ K 7 4	♡ K 7 4
◇ A 10 5 3	◇ A 10 5 3	◇ A 10 5 3
♣ J 10 2	♣ J 10 2	♣ K 10 2
Pass	2NT	3NT

You can think of the three possible actions by responder as red, amber and green. With 10 points or less he stops in 1NT, with 11 or 12 points he wants to invite opener to proceed if happy, and with 13+ he goes straight ahead and bids game at once.

Now consider responder holding an unbalanced hand with a suit of five cards or longer. When responder decides there is no game he has only two options, to leave 1NT by Passing, or remove to the long suit at the Two level. The response of, say, 2♡, to 1NT is NOT an exploring bid as you might expect from the simplest definition given earlier ('the first mention of a suit as trumps is exploratory') but a *sign-off*, naming the final contract. This is possible because the opening 1NT is such a descriptive bid. This response is called the 'weakness take-out of 1NT'. As the opener knows the bid is a sign-off responder can make a weakness take-out whenever he feels it is a better contract than 1NT.

For example, suppose you held as responder:

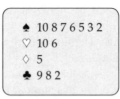

♠ 10 8 7 6 5 3 2
♡ 10 6
◇ 5
♣ 9 8 2

No high-card points at all and seven spades. 2♠ will be a better contract than 1NT (your hand will make three or four tricks with spade ruffs, instead of none when there are no trumps) even if both are destined to fail. Had partner opened 1♡ you must Pass because if you respond 1♠ (exploratory) not only must opener rebid, but also he will assume you hold six or more points and may rebid far too highly. But where your partner opens 1NT and you have the same hand you can make the weakness take-out of 2♠ secure in the knowledge that opener will Pass.

If you have a weak hand with a 6-card suit it is equally obvious to make the weakness take-out because opener's worst holding in the suit would be two cards, and that means you have the necessary for a satisfactory trump suit. If you had a weak hand with a 5-card suit you would be taking a slight gamble by making the weakness take-out (if opener has only two cards you are in a trump-fit of seven cards) but it is a gamble worth taking. Most of the time opener will have 3- or 4-card support, and even when he has only two, you will often find it easier to scramble a few trump tricks by ruffing rather than making them by power as you have to do when there are no trumps.

Now suppose responder has a hand with a long suit strong enough to open the bidding e.g.

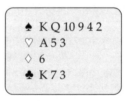

♠ K Q 10 9 4 2
♡ A 5 3
◇ 6
♣ K 7 3

If partner opens 1NT there must be a game on. Having six spades yourself, you know the partnership has at least eight spades between the two hands, and the obvious response would be 4♠, the game contract in spades. But if you only had five spades, you would like to know whether partner has more than two spades before committing yourself to 4♠ rather than 3NT. For example:

```
♠ K Q 6 3 2
♡ A 5 3
◊ J 6
♣ K 7 3
```

The solution is to respond 3♠. This is a *'jump-shift'*. In Acol, a jump-shift (bidding a new suit one level higher than necessary) traditionally indicates at least the values for game, but not necessarily the knowledge of which game. Partner must not Pass until a game contract is reached but can be involved in indicating which game is preferred. The jump-shift promises five cards in the suit named. Here, if opener held only two cards in spades, the worst possible, he would not Pass but would rebid 3NT to indicate he had only two cards in spades. If he held three or four cards in spades again he would not Pass however bad his hand, but would go on to 4♠.

The responses described so far are summarised in the table below:

Responses to the Opening 1NT			
Is there a game on?	**NO (0-10)**	**MAYBE (11-12)**	**YES (13+)**
Responder's hand			
Balanced shape	Pass	2NT	3NT
6-card suit (e.g. spades)	2♠		4♠
5-card suit (e.g. spades)	2♠		3♠
4-card suit (e.g. spades)	Pass		

There are several gaps in the chart. What do you do if you have an invitational hand with five or six spades? What if you have only four spades and wish to play in no-trumps unless opener happens to have four spades as well? The responses of 2♠, 3♠ and 4♠ are already in use to mean something else. The problems are solved by a convention called *Stayman* that is covered later in the book. A convention is a bid that by agreement between partners conveys a meaning other than the one you might expect. For the moment you have only the options shown in the table above.

If responder was happy with no-trumps and had as many as 21 points, he would know the partnership held at least 33 and would raise to 6NT. With 19 or 20 points, responder needs opener to be at the top end of the opening range to make the slam, and so raises to 4NT. As this is above the game contract of 3NT, opener realises it is an invitation to go on to 6NT if he is at the top end of the range.

Summary for 1NT Opening and Responses

- When partner opens 1NT, use his known point-count range to check whether, when added to your own, there is enough for game. Have it clear in your head: No, Maybe or Yes. If you are happy with no-trumps as the final denomination:

  > if the answer was No, Pass;
  > if the answer was Maybe, invite with 2NT;
  > if the answer was Yes, go straight to 3NT.

  Similarly, where responder wishes to invite a small slam, he can raise to 4NT. Opener will Pass with a strength at the bottom end of the range for the opening, but move on to 6NT when at the upper end of the range.

- After the 2NT invitation opener will Pass if his strength is at the lower end of the range for his opener, and go on to 3NT if his strength is at the upper end of the original range.

- If you want to suggest a suit as trumps (five cards or more) either make a weakness take-out into the suit at the two level (ending the auction) or make a jump-shift in the suit at the Three level. After the jump-shift partner will return to 3NT with only two cards in your suit, or raise with a better holding.

Exercises for 1NT Opening and Responses

Q1 Partner opens 1NT. What do you call holding:

	(a)	(b)	(c)
♠	K 9 4	A K 4	A K 4
♡	A 10 6	A J 6	A 6 3
◇	K Q 4 2	K Q 4 2	K Q 4 2
♣	A 8 3	A 8 3	A 8 3

A1 (a) 3NT; (b) 6NT; (c) 4NT. In (a) the answer to the question 'is there a game on?' is clearly 'yes' but even if partner held the maximum 14 points the partnership does not have enough for the next higher bonus contract (the small slam of 6NT requiring 33 points). So you bid 3NT. In (b) you have 21 high-card points so the partnership has at least 33, and you can go straight to 6NT, hoping for the slam bonus. In (c) you have slightly less, 20 points, and do not want to risk bidding 6NT in case opener has only 12 points, so you bid 4NT. The principle, as with the invitational raise to game of 2NT, is that your reason for going higher than the lower bonus level is that 'maybe' you can make the contract with the higher bonus, i.e. 4NT is an invitation to opener to bid 6NT if he is at the top end of the range, and pass 4NT otherwise.

Q2 You open 1NT with the hands below and partner responds 2NT. What is your rebid?

	(a)	(b)
♠	A 8 3	A Q 3
♡	K J 6 2	K J 6 2
◇	A 10 4	A 10 4
♣	10 9 3	10 9 3

A2 (a) Pass; (b) 3NT. You are being invited to go on to 3NT if you have the upper end of the range 12 to 14. In (a) you are at the bottom end of the range, so Pass. In (b), at the top end, accept the invitation to go 3NT, and don't worry about the clubs!

Q3 Partner opens 1NT. What would you call holding:

(a)	(b)	(c)
♠ A 8 3	♠ A 8 3	♠ A J 3
♡ K J 10 3 2	♡ Q 8 3	♡ A Q 3
◇ Q 6 3	◇ K J 5 3 2	◇ K J 10 6 4 2
♣ K 2	♣ K 2	♣ 2

A3 (a) 3♡; (b) 3NT; (c) 3◇. In each case the answer to the question 'Is there a game on?' is Yes. In the first case, where you hold a 5-card major, in this case hearts, make the jump-shift in hearts. If partner has 3 or 4 hearts he will raise to 4♡ which will probably be safer than 3NT. With only two hearts he will rebid 3NT and you should accept this and Pass 3NT. When your 5-card suit is a minor the alternative game to 3NT is at the Five level, two tricks more. As your hand is suitable for no-trumps and your strength is insufficient to expect 11 tricks, the only sensible call is 3NT. Don't make the jump-shift of 3◇ unless you want opener to raise you with diamond support, as in (c).

8

Two-Level Openings and Responses

In the Acol system used in this book opening bids at the two level are all strong and cover hands that are too strong to open at the one level. The reason for opening at the two level is that your hand is so strong that you fear, if you open at the one level, that the auction might end there and then with three Passes, and yet your side has a game contract available.

Consider balanced hands first. You need 25 or 26 points to make the game contract of 3NT. By 25 or 26 we mean, with 26 points you should definitely be in game, with 24 you should not reach game. With exactly 25 it won't matter too much whether you bid a game or not as it will have half-a-chance of success, but most prefer to be in game on that total.

When the opening bid is at the one level responder will Pass with fewer than six points. This means that when you have as many as 20 points, you should be thinking, 'if I open at the one level, partner will Pass with 5 points and we may have missed a game.' No-trump bids are limit bids with a 3-point range so the opening bid of 2NT shows 20-22 points. These hands would all be opened 2NT:

♠ A Q 5	♠ K 4	♠ Q 4	♠ 10 6 3
♡ K J 4 3	♡ A Q 2	♡ A Q	♡ A K J
♢ K Q 10	♢ K J 10 4 3	♢ K Q 10 2	♢ K Q J 3
♣ A Q 9	♣ A K 8	♣ A Q J 4 3	♣ A K J

An opening 1NT shows 12-14 points, so you may be wondering what you open with a balanced hand of between 15 and 19 points. The answer is that you must open with one of your long suits (every bridge hand has a 4-card or longer suit!) and bid no-trumps to show the balanced hand on the next round, as described in Chapter 4.

Opening at the Two level means there is less room to investigate but also simplifies the responses. If responder has a balanced hand of 5-10 points it is clear for him to raise 2NT to 3NT. With 3 points or less he will Pass, as the most the partnership can have is 25. But what if he holds exactly 4 points? He would like to make an invitational raise (such as 2NT over 1NT) where the opener goes on to game with a maximum and Passes with a minimum. Unfortunately, we are already in 2NT and are not permitted to bid 'Two-and-a-half No-trumps'. An invitational raise to game is not possible. Responder must either Pass the opening 2NT or commit the side to game.

After an opening of 2NT an invitational bid is possible where responder is thinking of slam. The partnership needs 33 points to justify bidding 6NT. Suppose as responder you hold 11 or 12 points and a balanced hand. You know the partnership has enough for slam if opener is at the top end of the range but not enough if he has the minimum. You can indicate this by raising to 4NT. If opener has a minimum 20 points he will Pass. With a maximum 22 points he can go on to 6NT. One might suppose that with exactly 21 opener can also sit on the fence by tottering on to 5NT, leaving the final decision to responder, but this idea is not included in standard Acol.

Now consider responder holding an unbalanced hand. The key situation is where he has a major suit of five or six cards. With a 6-card major and enough points for game, responder jumps straight to game, i.e. 4♡ or 4♠. With a 5-card major responder wants to suggest that suit as trumps, and leave opener to decide whether to go for game in the major or 3NT. Responder can only do this by bidding his suit at the three level. This is a more important role for the bid than having a weakness take-out to 2NT. After an opening 1NT a suit bid at the two level is the weakness take-out and opener Passes. There is NO WEAKNESS TAKE-OUT to an opening 2NT. Any new suit bid is exploratory and the opener must not Pass. Instead the opener raises or returns to 3NT depending on which game he thinks stands a better chance. The main determining factor is the number of cards opener has in responder's suit. With only two cards he will normally reject the proposal of that suit as trumps and choose 3NT.

Here is a table summarising the responses to the opening 2NT:

Responses to the Opening 2NT				
Responder's range	0-3	4-10	11-12	13+
Responder's hand				
Balanced	Pass	3NT	4NT	6NT
6-card major	Pass	4 of the suit	See text	6 of the suit
5-card major	Pass	3 of the suit	See text	See text

See if you can work out for yourself what you might do as responder with a 5- or 6-card major and a hand that wanted to invite slam. You could bid the suit at the three level to find out whether opener liked it or not (remember, opener cannot Pass this exploratory response) and then move on over opener's rebid, but without going to slam. Opener should realise you have interest in slam.

Enough about responding to 2NT. We turn to the opening bids of 2♠, 2♡ and 2◇ (the special case of 2♣ will be dealt with at the end of the chapter). These are exploratory bids with a wider range of strength than 3 points. The point count might be described as 20-24 but for powerful and highly distributional hands there is a better measure, namely the number of tricks they can be expected to win if partner has a useless hand. You will find that if you can make eight tricks with no help from partner, then if partner has actually has a useful king and queen (5 points) together you have enough for game.

Also, as room for investigation has been reduced, we require the opening bid at the Two level to promise at least five cards in the suit named, rather than the minimum of four shown by an opening bid at the one level. This means responder will only need three cards in the suit for the partnership to have the magic 8-card fit. But it also creates the problem of what to open holding a powerful hand with three 4-card suits and a singleton. The singleton prohibits opening 2NT, and the length of the suits prohibits opening Two of a suit. You are left with opening one of your cheapest suit, and hoping the auction does not stop there. This is an awkward hand in the Acol system but fortunately it is a rare shape to pick up, so don't worry about it too much.

To summarise, an opening at the two level promises at least five cards in the suit named, and either 20 points or the ability to make eight tricks without help from partner. These hands would all be opened 2♡:

♠ 4	♠ A	♠ A 6 3
♡ A K Q 8 7 3	♡ A K J 10 4	♡ K Q J 10 5 4
◇ A K 3	◇ A K J 3 2	◇ 3
♣ K 4 2	♣ 7 4	♣ A K J

Now suppose you picked up this hand as dealer:

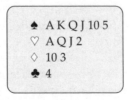

♠ A K Q J 10 5
♡ A Q J 2
◇ 10 3
♣ 4

You count 17 HCP and 2 long-suit points, not enough, it seems, to justify opening at the Two level. But it is clear that the traditional point count undervalues that spade suit, which can be expected to win six tricks whatever dummy offers. You can see the hand will take eight tricks (six in spades and two in hearts) without any real help from partner. Furthermore, if partner happens to hold the king of hearts, that will give you an easy ten tricks and therefore game with spade as trumps. So the hand is strong enough to open 2♠. The point count method could be justified by saying that with a powerful self-sufficient suit like the one illustrated you can immediately upgrade the hand for the short suits (one point for the doubleton and two for the singleton). This would bring the valuation up to 22 points, similar to counting it as eight tricks.

Here is another strong hand to evaluate:

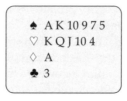

The point count is 17 HCP and 3 long-suit points, making the 20 that suggests a Two level opening. And the hand can be expected to make eight tricks even if dummy has no high cards. Indeed, if dummy put down as little as four small spades or four small hearts you should expect to make game in the major suit for which responder has support. If he has four hearts and few spades then, with hearts as trumps, you should be able to trump one or two spades in dummy, removing all the opponents' cards in the suit and leaving the rest as winners.

As this is a common feature of a hand with two powerful suits the Acol system adopts the practice that responder should not Pass an exploratory opening at the Two level even if he has no high-card points at all. He must respond to the opening in order to give the strong hand a chance to mention a second powerful suit should it have one. Responder may have enough to give the partnership game in the second suit, of which he would not have heard without the initial response.

But hang on a minute! If responder is compelled to make a bid even with a lousy hand, how can opener know when responder actually has enough strength to justify bidding normally? The solution to this problem brings us to an important new aspect of bidding. It is the idea of an artificial bid, one that does not mean what it appears to mean, called a convention. On its first appearance it needs an introductory explanation including some relevant points in the Laws.

The Laws of Bridge do not specify what information is conveyed by bids. It is the player who agrees with partner that the strength of their opening 1NT, for example, shows a balanced hand of 12 to 14 HCP. The Laws say that such agreements are allowed but must not be secret. The opponents are entitled to know what agreements players have with their partners about the meaning conveyed by their bids. Players may even ask an opponent what their bids mean. It is usually best to leave this to the end of the auction, though the Laws permit you to do this when it is your turn to call. Of course, no other player has the right to be told what your HAND is. To find that out is the main point of the game. So the rule is that only the partner of the bidder, the one who cannot see the hand, explains what agreement they have about the meaning of the bid.

As the Laws do not say what bids mean, might you agree that a particular bid meant 'It is my turn to buy the drinks, please tell me via your next bid, what you want'? One response could mean 'Beer, please', another 'wine' etc. Well, it might be legal but it would not be useful, as such questions and answers are permitted verbally in addition to your bids. But it is both legal and useful to have a bid meaning 'I have a bad hand', and that is what the Acol system uses in response to an exploratory Two of a suit opening. Note that methods of showing a bad hand other than via your bids, for example, by looking glum or disinterested, are forbidden by the Laws!

In Acol the response of 2NT to an opening 2♠, 2♡ or 2◇, does NOT mean 'I have a balanced hand', as you might expect, but 'I have a bad hand', usually fewer than 7 points. The call has two advantages. It gives the strong hand a chance to show a second suit if it has one, and it serves to dampen the enthusiasm of the strong hand for a slam, directing that player back to the routine matter of game or part-score. The 2NT response is called the Negative Response. Note that if the opponent in between had bid then the opener would automatically have another chance to speak, and responder could simply, as normal, Pass to show a bad hand. 2NT would become natural, with a stop in the opponent's suit and an otherwise balanced hand.

The Laws restrict the use of artificial bids. The opponents are entitled to know but you are not allowed to remind your partner that a call is artificial. So both members of a partnership need to remember the unusual meaning if a potentially disastrous misunderstanding is to be avoided. The Laws also allow the organisers of an event to license or limit the number and type of artificial agreements a partnership uses. The restrictions will reflect the standard of the event. In World Championships most artificial bids are allowed but you have to give advance notice of them to your opponents. In a Beginners' event very few artificial bids will be permitted, but those described in this book are likely to be allowed in any bridge tournament.

An analogy from golf is the rule specifying the maximum number of clubs a player may carry in their bag. The differing clubs are an artificial but permitted aid to accuracy, and a player is limited in the number allowed. A golfer may not be followed by a lorry carrying a hundred different clubs, and bridge ceases to be a fair game of deduction unless players are restricted in their use of artificial calls.

As the negative response of 2NT is artificial opener must not Pass it. He can show a second suit, or repeat the first with extra length (i.e. at least six cards). Responder's continuations are natural.

A responder who does not use the negative response is known to have at least seven points. Consider the simple auction: 2♠ (Pass) 3♠.

This may look like a limit bid from the responder, but a moment's thought will give a different interpretation. Opener has the equivalent of at least 20 points and responder has at least seven, so the partnership has at least 27, enough for game. So the raise cannot be Passed by the opener and it is not a limit bid. Responder is simply indicating that he agrees spades will be trumps, and may even be interested in slam.

So, where both players know the partnership has enough for game there are no limit bids below that level. Contrast the two auctions: 2♠ – 3♣ – 3♠ and 2♠ – 2NT – 3♠.

In the first, responder has given a positive response so the partnership is in what is called a *game-forcing* auction. Opener's repeat of spades shows extra length (at least six) but is not a limit bid. But in the second, as the response was the negative, the partnership is not known to have game values. The rebid still shows six spades but it is a limit bid, showing an eight trick hand, and can be Passed. Note, however, that if responder had as few as five points he would still be expected to move on to game, because the reason for opening at the two level was that five points opposite would provide the values for game. For example, you hold:

♠ 10 9 4
♡ A 9 4 2
♢ 9 6 4 2
♣ 6 3

If partner had opened 1♠ you, having fewer than 6 points, would Pass. But when partner opens 2♠, first give the negative 2NT to warn partner you have a poor hand, and on the next round go to 4♠ as you have 3-card support and actually a good hand within the context of your initial negative response.

We now deal with the opening bid of 2♣. What can you open with a balanced hand of more than 22 points? If you had 23 or 24 points that would not be quite enough to justify 3NT, and even if you had 25 or 26 HCP and could happily open 3NT, the snag would be that you have lost two levels of exploratory bidding that, depending on partner's hand, might suggest a suit contract or a slam. Consider also the possibility that you pick up a hand so powerful that it will make game whatever strength partner has, but which game will depend on the number of cards he has in each suit. For example, you hold:

♠ A K 9 8 4
♡ A K Q 2
◇ A K J
♣ Q

You have 26 HCP and 1 length point, enough to expect to make game opposite any old rubbish, but which game? If partner has three spades, 4♠ will be a suitable spot. If partner has four hearts, then 4♡ is the game. If partner has fewer than three spades and fewer than four hearts, but has at least five diamonds, then diamonds is the right denomination. And finally, if he has fewer than three spades, fewer than four hearts, and fewer than five diamonds, he must have clubs, and 3NT could well be the best spot.

On such a hand not only do you want to keep exploring even when partner has no points, but you also would like to tell him your hand is so strong that even a modest hand opposite might provide a slam.

For these reasons all systems contain one opening at not too high a level that has no upper limit in strength. In the Acol system this is the opening bid of 2♣. This is a completely artificial bid. The bidder is too powerful to open with any other call. He may have a balanced hand of 23-24 points or any hand with the equivalent of 25 points, balanced or not.

You can have any shape of hand to open 2♣, even a hand that has no clubs at all. In bridge it is a rare for a pundit to say accurately 'Always' or 'Never'. There are usually several exceptions to any rule. But here we can say it forcefully. If your partner opens 2♣ and the opponent to your right says Pass, you must NEVER, EVER Pass. For one thing, if you did, it would be the surest way to lose a good friend. Your partner is looking at the best hand he has seen in months, an array of aces and kings that have made game a near certainty and perhaps slam a likelihood. If the final contract was 2♣ with him as declarer, possibly with no clubs in his hand, and his high cards being trumped with glee by the opponents, expect worse than a frosty glare.

So you must respond to 2♣ even with zero points. The system must specify a negative response. In Acol this is 2◇. (2NT as a negative over 2♣ would waste too much space needed for exploration, and frequently the finally contract will be 3NT, better played with the opening lead to the left of the hand with all the high cards.) So when the auction has gone 2♣ – 2◇, the opener has said: 'I have a very powerful hand', at least 23 points, and responder has said: 'I have a weak hand', fewer than 7. But from then on all bids are natural. Note the very different fears the two partners have that are now out of the way. The opener, with the wonderful hand, fears that if he takes the bidding step-by-step to describe the shape of his hand, responder with the lousy hand may Pass before they reach game. Responder, by contrast, with the weak hand, fears that if he keeps on bidding as required, partner may put him with a better hand and leap to some unmakeable slam. Provided both partners recall the initial artificial bids such mishaps are avoided.

If after the start 2♣ – 2◊ the opener rebids 2NT he would be showing a balanced hand of 23-24 points. This is the only sequence that starts with 2♣ but can stop short of game. If responder had really nothing, at most a queen, he could Pass, but anything better and he will keep going exactly as if his partner had opened 2NT.

All other sequences starting with 2♣ must end in at least game. For example, if the auction started 2♣ – 2♡ – 2NT responder has a positive response of at least 7 points with hearts as his longest suit. Opener shows a balanced hand but it is not a limit bid as both players know they are going to at least game.

Similarly if the start was: 2♣ – 2◊ – 2♠ responder has given the negative and may have zero points, but opener's continuation in a new suit is game-forcing. Responder must keep going, showing his shape naturally until game is reached. Here is an example using the hand given earlier:

```
    ♠ A K 9 8 4              ♠ 4
    ♡ A K Q 2        N      ♡ J 8 7 3
    ◊ A K J        W   E    ◊ 8 5 3
    ♣ Q              S      ♣ 9 7 6 5 3
```

The auction should go: 2♣ – 2◊ – 2♠ – 3♣ – 3♡ – 4♡ – Pass.

As the opening 2♣ includes all hands with game values there is an upper limit to the opening 2♠, 2♡ and 2◊ of about 24 points or nine tricks.

A snag of all conventions is that when a bid has an artificial meaning you lose its natural meaning. So what can you open with a hand of 20 points and clubs as the longest suit? You cannot open it 2♣. Instead you must either open 2NT or, if that is not feasible, open 1♣ and hope the auction does not end there. Similarly, what if partner opens 2♣, and, in response, you have diamonds as your longest suit with positive values such as 9 points? Answer: you must respond 3◊. This may sound like a jump-shift, but really it is not. 3◊ was the lowest level at which you could bid the suit naturally.

Summary of Two-Level Openings and Responses

- In the Acol system all opening bids at the Two level are hands too strong to open at the one level. If your hand is so strong that there is a danger an opening bid by you at the one level can be Passed by partner with a hand that will easily provide a game contract, then you should consider opening at the Two level.

- The opening bid of 2NT shows a hand balanced in shape with 20-22 points. There is no weakness take-out. A response at the three level in a suit is exploratory and promises at least five cards in the suit named. Opener may go back to 3NT (and should do so with only two cards in the suit), or raise responder's suit with 3- or 4-card support. Responder's raise to 4NT is invitational to 6NT with opener Passing only when his hand is at the lower end of the range for the opening.

- An opening bid of 2♠, 2♡, or 2◊ shows at least five cards in the suit named and a strength equivalent to 20-24 points, or eight or nine tricks without help from partner. Partner must respond and, with a strength of fewer than 7 points, bids 2NT, the artificial negative.

- An opening bid of 2♣ is completely artificial showing a hand of unlimited strength too strong to open anything else. It is either a balanced hand of 23-24 points, or any hand of game-going strength, balanced or unbalanced. The negative response is 2◊. All rebids by opener are game-forcing except 2NT showing 23-24 balanced.

Exercises for Two-Level Openings and Responses

How should these two hands be bid, with West the Dealer and the opponents passing throughout? Assess the prospects for the final contract.

Q1

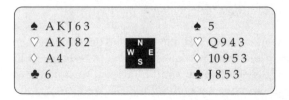

♠ A K J 6 3	♠ 5
♡ A K J 8 2	♡ Q 9 4 3
◇ A 4	◇ 10 9 5 3
♣ 6	♣ J 8 5 3

A1 West has 20 HCP and 2 long-suit points, and should open 2♠ – the higher of two 5-card suits. East, who would have Passed an opening bid of 1♠ having only 3 HCP, now gives the negative response of 2NT. West rebids 3♡ to show his second suit, and East, having upgraded his hand by 2 points for the heart fit and singleton spade, happily raises to 4♡. The full auction is:

West	East
2♠	2NT
3♡	4♡
Pass	

In the play West should plan to trump at least two small spades in the dummy. Hopefully, the last spade will then become a winner. West must lose a club and a diamond, and maybe one more, but probably makes 11 tricks. Suppose the defence start with the two rounds of clubs. West ruffs the second, at once plays ace of spades, trump a spade, then returns to hand with a trump. Provided both defenders follow the trumps cannot be worse than 3-1, so West can trump another spade with the queen of hearts, and draw trumps. The contract has 10 easy tricks and an eleventh unless one defender held five spades to the queen.

Q2

```
♠ K J 5              ♠ Q 4 3
♡ A Q         N      ♡ 10 8 4
◇ J 7 3     W   E    ◇ Q 9 4 2
♣ A K Q 6 3   S      ♣ J 8 4
```

A2 West has 20 HCP and 1 long-suit point and should open 2NT,
showing a balanced hand of 20-22. West must not open 2♣ which
would be the artificial bid showing a stronger hand, and any shape.
East, who would have Passed an opening one bid having only 5
points, raises 2NT to 3NT.

Unless the clubs are 5-0 declarer can count five club tricks, two
spades and a heart for eight tricks. The ninth will come from either
the heart finesse (succeeding when South has the king) or a helpful
red suit lead.

♠ ♡ ◇ ♣

Q3

```
♠ A K 3              ♠ 8 5 2
♡ K Q 4       N      ♡ J 10 9 7 3
◇ A K J 9 3  W   E   ◇ Q 7 2
♣ K 2         S      ♣ 8 3
```

A3 With 23 HCP and 1 long-suit point West is too strong for 2NT. As the
hand is balanced in character an opening bid of 2♣ (planning to
rebid 2NT) is more descriptive than an opening 2◇ bid. To an
opening 2♣ East responds 2◇, the artificial negative. West, as
planned rebids 2NT, showing 23-24. East has enough to bid on, and
should show the 5-card heart suit by bidding 3♡. This is not a
weakness take-out, but exploratory and *forcing*, asking West to
choose between 4♡ and 3NT as a contract. West, with 3-card support
should raise to 4♡.

4♡ is significantly superior to 3NT. 3NT fails if the defence find a
club lead, even though West makes the king. Eventually the defence
gain the lead with the ace of hearts to cash at least four clubs. Even
if the defence lead a spade, South may hold the ace of hearts and
switch to a club, West must try the club king and pray North does
not have the ace, or the game will fail by more than one trick.

By contrast, in 4♡, West wins any lead as soon as possible and starts
on drawing trumps by playing the king. When next on lead, West

draws the remaining trumps and then plays diamonds. The game should make in comfort.

Q4 In these auctions describe the meaning of East's bid of 2♣:

	West	North	East	South
(a)	1♣	Pass	2♣	
(b)	1♠	Pass	2♣	
(c)	Pass	Pass	2♣	

A4 (a) 6-9 points and 4+ clubs;
    (b) 9+ points, 4+ clubs, fewer than 4♠;
    (c) 23-24 points balanced or a game-going hand of any shape.

9

Both Sides Bidding

So far, nearly every auction given has involved only one partnership. The other side has been sitting there saying Pass throughout. Real life is not like that. If you watch high standard bridge (and these days you can watch bridge free of charge on the internet from the comfort of your own home) more than half the auctions have both sides bidding.

A bridge match can be just as exciting to watch as any physical sport. The format is the same whether you play for fun at home, or it is the final of the world championships. A match is a contest between two teams of four players each. Two tables play the same deals. At one table the 'Home' team sits North-South, with the 'Away' team East-West, and at the other the positions are reversed, as shown:

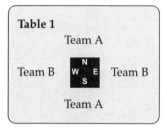
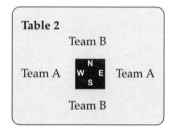

Each deal constitutes one little contest. When the same deal has been played at both tables the two teams have held identical cards. What matters is the difference between the score at the two tables. This is called the 'swing' on the deal. The swing is normally converted into 'match points' and these swings are added through all the deals to determine the winner. The final of the world championships can be as many as 160 deals or 'boards', taking three days to play, but in Monte Carlo in 2003, in a 128-board final between the USA and Italy the outcome was still only decided on the last card played of the last deal played.

On the internet, you can watch events such as the World or European Championships, or the British Home Internationals, with your national team in play. Unlike the players, you can see all four hands. There is a commentary to explain bids that you might not understand and what options the players are considering. After each deal is played, the players know the result at their own table but not what happened at the other table. So bridge is unique in one respect: the spectators actually know the result of the match before the players at the table. You can know who has become the new world champion before the player does!

You will see that bidding is not merely a constructive exercise, where the side with better cards is trying to reach the highest-scoring contract for its partnership. It is also a competitive exercise, where both sides can make a decent contract of their own, or even sometimes a destructive one, where the side with the lesser values is trying to prevent the other side finding its best contract. At the end of the play, if they are writing down a score of +620, you are writing down –620. If instead you record a score of –300 failing in your own contract you have actually done better than leaving them to find and make their optimum contract.

Furthermore you will see that experts act very differently on what are called the good-fit deals from what are termed *misfits*. By 'good fit' we mean North can support the same suit as South, and East can support the same suit as West. By misfit we mean North has different suits to South and their suits are each well held by an opponent. If one side has ten hearts between them, and the other side has ten spades, expect some very lively bidding. But if North has a suit or suits shown by an opponent expect an expert North to bid much more cautiously.

Compare these two auctions at two tables in a match playing the same deal:

Table 1			
West	**North**	**East**	**South**
1♡	Pass	2♡	All Pass

Table 2			
West	**North**	**East**	**South**
1♡	1♠	2♡	2♠
?			

At the first table West opened 1♡ to show 12-19 points with hearts as his longest suit. East raised to 2♡ showing 6-9 points and at least four hearts. West judged there was not enough to make 4♡, and so Passed 2♡, a comfortable contract that we may suppose made eight or nine tricks for his side.

The West at the second table made the same opening 1♡, but then North *overcalled* 1♠. East made the same raise to 2♡, but South *competed* to 2♠. Here West has a difficult decision. He can still judge his side cannot make 4♡ but has to choose whether to go to 3♡, a contract that might fail, or let the opponents play 2♠ when he is not sure whether that will succeed or fail. The intervention of North-South, even though they could judge 4♠ could not succeed, made life more difficult for East-West.

The side that opens the bidding more often than not is the side with the superior values, but it still pays for the other side to compete. So the values needed for an overcall at the one level are set one trick fewer than for an opening, i.e. the range for North's 1♠ overcall is more like 9-16 points (counting high cards and long-suit points, with 9 as a borderline case) rather than the 12-19 for an opening at the one level (with 12 as a borderline case). However to bid with lesser values is risky and to compensate you must have at least FIVE cards in the suit named.

If North's longest suit had been clubs, the lowest level he could overcall in the suit would be 2♣, an undertaking to make eight tricks. North would need at least 12 points AND at least five clubs to make the overcall.

Other factors influence good players in whether they overcall. Of these the quality of the suit is perhaps the most important (you can take a greater risk with a decent 5-card suit than a poor one). Negative points might be the vulnerability (if vulnerable, the penalty for failure is twice as great) and values in the opponents' suit (suggesting the deal may be a misfit).

West opens 1♡. North should overcall 1♠ with any of these hands:

♠ K Q J 8 7 3	♠ K J 10 9 3	♠ Q J 9 8 4
♡ 6	♡ 8 3	♡ A 5
◇ Q 8 3	◇ A J 3	◇ K Q 8 2
♣ 10 4 2	♣ 10 4 2	♣ K 3
8 HCP	**9 HCP**	**15 HCP**
2 long-suit	**1 long-suit**	**1 long-suit**

West opens 1♡. North should overcall 2♣ with any of these hands:

♠ 8 6	♠ 8 6	♠ K 4
♡ A 5	♡ 5 3	♡ 5 3
◇ K 9 4	◇ A K 6 2	◇ A Q 3
♣ A J 10 8 3 2	♣ K Q J 10 4	♣ K Q J 8 4 3
12 HCP	**13 HCP**	**15 HCP**
2 long-suit	**1 long-suit**	**2 long-suit**

How should partner respond to an overcall at the one level? As the overcall promised five cards in the suit named, *advancer* (that's the technical name for the overcaller's partner) only needs three cards in that suit to have the magic eight. As the overcall shows a trick fewer than an opening, advancer must be more cautious in exploring, but, with support for overcaller's suit, can certainly compete quite freely on the basis of pushing the opponents around a bit!

What does a jump overcall mean? In the Acol system it means a hand too strong to overcall at the one level and with a decent six card suit. When West opens 1♡, using the Acol agreements, North would overcall 2♠ with a hand like this:

```
♠ K Q J 8 7 3
♡ A 7 3
◇ A 5
♣ K 3
```

Note this also shows a range in strength about one trick fewer than an opening 2♠.

Now imagine West as dealer opens 1♡, and you as North are considering making an overcall of 1NT. As usual it shows a balanced hand. Can you do it with a trick fewer than an opening? No way! In fact this overcall shows a hand that is a trick better than a minimum opening, i.e. 15-17 HCP rather than 12-14. The reason is that to announce a balanced hand after the other side has opened the bidding is one of the riskiest actions in bidding.

To see this, suppose you are East, in third seat, with an average hand of ten points. The bidding has started:

West	North	East	South
1♡	1NT	?	

What do you know? Partner has 12 or more points so your side has at least 22, significantly more than half the points in the pack. North has said he will take more than half the tricks, holding a balanced hand, and you know his side has fewer than the half the points. You can immediately deduce North is out of his depth. You can 'double' and expect North to fail by at least two tricks.

Contrast that with the situation where North has overcalled 1♠. You have the same information about the point count, but you do not know how many spades North has. If he has a 6-card suit and finds support from his partner, South, in spades, they may easily make 7 tricks with spades as trumps, despite having significantly fewer than half the points. Only if you, East, held good spades would you know that North could not make his contract.

So, to risk an overcall of 1NT, North must hold a balanced hand of 15-17 points. He must also have a trick in the suit opened by the opponent (said to be a 'stop in their suit'). West has at least four hearts, perhaps six. East will lead what he knows to be West's best suit, and unless North can win a heart trick the opponents might rattle off six tricks in hearts before North can get the lead.

West opens 1♡. North should overcall 1NT on any of these hands:

♠ A Q 4	♠ K 4	♠ A 6
♡ K J 4	♡ A Q	♡ Q J 8 3
♢ K Q 10 4	♢ K J 6 3 2	♢ K J 3
♣ Q 6 2	♣ Q 10 4 3	♣ A Q 5 3

On the second of those hands you might have considered an overcall of 2♢ but 1NT is much more descriptive. You have the right point count, a double-stop in the opponent's suit (hearts), a balanced hand, and only a poor 5-card suit in diamonds.

Although the overcall of 1NT in second seat is very risky ('sandwiched' between the opener and the unknown strength of the other opponent), in fourth seat the risk disappears if responder has Passed as in the auction below:

West	North	East	South
1♡	Pass	Pass	1NT

Here East is known to have fewer than 6 points, so South's bid of 1NT can be made with merely a minimum opening hand as usual, i.e. 12-14 points. Indeed, because North, when fearing a misfit, might have Passed with quite a good hand with values in the opponent's suit, hearts, it is common practice, in fourth seat (said to be 'protecting partner's Pass') to bid with as few as 10 points even when balanced. We recommend you assume the protective 1NT shows 11-14.

Next we must consider what you do if you were planning to open the same suit as is actually opened by the opponent:

West opens 1♡ and North holds:

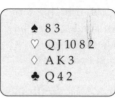

```
    ♠ 8 3
    ♡ Q J 10 8 2
    ◇ A K 3
    ♣ Q 4 2
```

If West had Passed, North would have opened 1♡. If West had opened 1♣ or 1◇, North would have overcalled 1♡. But what if West opens 1♡?

Does North 'Double' to indicate the same suit as West? No! The best tactic without a doubt is to say 'Pass.' The deal may well be a misfit. It would be wrong to warn them of that. On a misfit hand it is the side that keeps quiet that ends up smelling of roses. Here North should Pass and if the opponents reach 4♡, North will be happy to 'Double.' He expects them to lose a couple of diamond tricks and maybe three heart tricks. The double increases the size of the penalty suffered by East-West, i.e. a plus for North-South. That is a perfectly fair tactic even when their 4♡ contract is a sensible one with eight hearts between them and 26 points, ruined by the unlucky 5-0 break in hearts.

So, unless you have enough to make an overcall of 1NT, the best tactic, having the same suit as the opponent, is to keep quiet. Once bridge players realised this they stopped doubling opening bids of one of a suit. And that meant 'double' could be used to mean something else.

Suppose you hold this hand as North, second to speak:

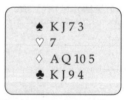

```
    ♠ K J 7 3
    ♡ 7
    ◇ A Q 10 5
    ♣ K J 9 4
```

You have counted your points (14) and are just trying to remember whether to open 1♠, 1◇, or 1♣ (1♠ would clearly be wrong as you have no sensible rebid if partner responds 2♡, 1♣ is reasonable, 1◇ is the action recommended by this book), when in the midst of your thoughts you hear West open 1♡. What now?

Do you want to bid? Yes, certainly. The hand may well be a good-fit hand with your partner being able to support one of your suits. (By contrast, had West opened 1♠ it would definitely be right to Pass as you suspect a misfit.) Snag. Any overcall in a suit promises five cards in the suit named, and you don't have a 5-card suit. And you certainly cannot overcall 1NT (you don't have the 15-17 strength, the balanced shape, or the trick in their suit!). You would be stymied but for an idea thought of in about 1912 in the days of auction bridge.

The idea was to give 'double' of an opening one of a suit the meaning 'I have enough points to justify bidding, but I want you, partner, to select the trump suit'. Problem solved. This means, of course, select a denomination other than the one already chosen by the opponent. Partner may only Pass the contract of 1♡ Doubled when he knows, holding a fistful of cards in their suit, that, unexpectedly, this is a good spot for your side. He must not Pass merely because he has a bad hand. If he did that the opener could also Pass, ending the auction. Opener, our opponent, would reap a rich reward by scoring up 1♡ Doubled with overtricks. So partner, even with a bad hand, must do as requested and select a trump suit.

As partner must select a trump suit even with a lousy hand, the doubler will then certainly Pass with any minimum double of 13-15 points (you may be too high already). And you need partner to make some value-showing response with 9 or more points to allow you to bid on happily with 16. All new suit bids in response to a take-out double are treated as limit bids, because the doubler is expected to have 3 or 4 card support in the suit.

The idea of what is called 'the take-out double' was so useful that players quickly extended its use from the rare hands with 4-card support for every other suit. The meaning became: 'I have at least 13 points and 3 or 4 cards in every suit other than the one opened by the opponent.' It was therefore often short of the suit opened by the opponent. Players also realised it could be used on hands that were too strong for a simple overcall, but the suit was not good enough for a jump overcall. Partner would show his best suit in response to the take-out double and then the doubler would continue exploring to show a hand too good for a simple overcall.

When West opens 1♡, North would double holding any of these hands:

♠ A Q 5 3	♠ A Q 5 3	♠ A Q 10 9 2
♡ 7 3	♡ 7	♡ 4 2
◇ A Q 4	◇ A K J 4	◇ A K J 4
♣ J 10 3 2	♣ A 8 7 3	♣ A 7

On the first the doubler would be Passing almost any response by partner. On the second doubler would raise the new suit bid by partner, and on the third doubler would continue over a response of 2♣ or 2◇ with 2♠ to show a hand too strong to overcall 1♠ and with a suit not good enough to overcall 2♠ initially.

What if the opening by West was 1NT rather than one of a suit? The double cannot be take-out in the sense that it shows shortness in the opponent's suit with support for the other three, because the opponent has not bid a suit. The meaning is simply: 'I have a better hand than that shown by the opener,' i.e. if the remaining points are shared equally between the other two players, the contract of 1NT should fail. The double is therefore described as a 'penalty double' even though the doubler does not necessarily have enough in his own hand to defeat the opponent's 1NT. Note that you are allowed to know the strength of the opening 1NT and can ask the opponent to your left (not the one who opened) what strength they have agreed it shows. If it shows 12-14 as in Acol, then your double will show 15+. If it showed, say, 14-16, your double should have 17.

When 1NT is doubled the next two players can be given the same advice. With a balanced hand leave the contract as 1NT doubled. With a weak hand and a 5-card suit remove to the safety of that suit (a weakness take-out).

Summary of Both Sides Bidding

- An overcall in a suit at the one level shows 9-16 points and a 5-card suit. At the two level it shows 12-17 and a 5-card suit. The overcall of 1NT shows a balanced hand of 15-17 points with a stop in their suit. A jump overcall shows a hand too good to overcall at the one level with a decent 6-card suit. Double is for take-out, showing at least 13 points and either 3 or 4 cards in every other suit or a hand too strong to make a simple overcall but with a suit not good enough to make a jump overcall.
  With a minimum opening hand and strength in the suit bid by the opponent, Pass.

- When advancing partner's overcall, 3-card support is sufficient for a raise. Act cautiously without a fit in partner's suit, and progressively more boldly the better the support you have for partner. If partner makes a take-out double, only Pass when you have great length in the opponent's suit and are therefore happy with the contract as it is. Do not Pass with a bad hand, instead follow partner's request and select a trump suit (or no-trumps with some values in their suit and a balanced hand).

- When the opening is 1NT, double shows a hand stronger than the opponent's hand. The other two players should Pass with balanced hands. The time to remove 1NT to 2 of a suit is when you have a weak hand with a 5-card suit.

Exercises for Both Sides Bidding

Q1 West opens 1♢. You are North, second to speak, vulnerable against not. What do you call with these hands?

(a)	(b)	(c)
♠ A 4	♠ A 4	♠ A 4
♡ Q J 9 8 3	♡ K 3 2	♡ K 3 2
♢ 4 3	♢ Q J 4 3	♢ Q 4 3
♣ K 6 3 2	♣ K 6 3 2	♣ K 6 5 3 2

(d)	(e)	(f)
♠ A 4	♠ A J 3	♠ A Q 10 7 3
♡ K 3 2	♡ K 6 3 2	♡ A 6
♢ Q J 3	♢ 3 2	♢ 3 2
♣ K Q 9 3 2	♣ K Q 3 2	♣ A K J 2

A1 (a) 10 HCP, and a decent 5-card suit. A sound overcall of 1♡.

(b) 13 HCP, no 5-card suit, and values in their suit. Pass.

(c) 12 HCP and a 5-card suit. So you overcall 2♣? No. Your judgment should be telling you to Pass, particularly as you are vulnerable. The 5-card suit is a poor one to be bidding at the Two level. And the queen in their suit is not good news for attack.

(d) 15 HCP and a 5-card suit. So you overcall 2♣? Well, you have the values, but 1NT would be a much better description of your hand. For a 1 NT overcall, you have the right point count (15-17), a balanced shape, and values in their suit.

(e) 13 HCP, no wasted values in their suit, and 3 or 4 cards in every other suit. Double.

(f) 18 HCP and a decent 5-card suit. You are too strong to make a simple overcall, but the suit is not good enough to overcall 2♠. Double and over any response by partner continue exploring by bidding your spade suit.

♠ ♡ ♢ ♣

Q2 West opens 1♡, North, now your partner, overcalls 1♠, East Passes. What do you call as South, holding these hands?:

(a)	(b)	(c)	(d)	(e)
♠ Q93	♠ 43	♠ 43	♠ K6532	♠ 43
♡ 43	♡ J93	♡ K103	♡ 3	♡ J73
◇ 732	◇ Q732	◇ Q932	◇ A843	◇ Q32
♣ AJ842	♣ A842	♣ AQ53	♣ Q103	♣ KJ742

A2. (a) 7 HCP, a 5-card minor and 3-card support for partner's major. As the overcall promises five cards, raise to 2♠ despite the range being 3 points less. As you know your side has eight spades this is superior to Passing (allowing a cheap re-entry to opener). To mention the clubs you would need more points and fewer spades.

(b) 7 HCP, no long suit, and less than 3-card support for partner. Pass.

(c) 11 HCP, a balanced hand, and values in the opponent's suit. Respond 1NT, being more cautious than you would in response to an opening bid, as the overcall only shows 9-16 points.

(d) 9 HCP, 1 long-suit point and 2 for the singleton heart. Certainly worth 3♠ but your judgement should be telling you to bid Four. The known 10-card fit and singleton in their suit both suggest stretching for the game.

(e) 7 HCP and a 5-card suit, but it is a minor suit and you have less than 3-card support for partner. Pass.

Q3 West opens 1♡, North, your partner, doubles, East Passes. What do you call, holding?:

(a)	(b)	(c)	(d)	(e)
♠ 10 7 4 3	♠ 10 7 4	♠ A Q 5 3	♠ A Q 5 3 2	♠ 4 3
♡ 4 3	♡ Q 10 8 2	♡ 4 3	♡ 4	♡ Q J 10 9 3 2
◊ 9 8 3	◊ J 6 3	◊ 9 8 3	◊ 9 8 3	◊ A 2
♣ Q 4 3 2	♣ A 8 3	♣ K 4 3 2	♣ A 4 3 2	♣ 9 7 3

A3 (a) A miserable hand but partner's take-out double requests you to select a trump suit and you must do so. The clubs may be better than the spades, but the correct response is 1♠. That has the advantage of keeping the bidding a level lower, and if partner has only 13 points you may already be too high.

(b) 7 HCP, a balanced hand, and values in the opponent's suit. Bid 1NT.

(c) 9 HCP, and a decent 4-card major. Jump to 2♠. This is not a jump-shift (partner has already promised 3 or 4 spades). It is a limit bid, bearing in mind that partner may have only three spades but unless you jump he won't know you have any points at all. (See your response in (a).)

(d) 10 HCP, 1 long-suit point and 2 short-suit points (you expect to have 8 spades between you), a total of 13. Partner has 13+. Bid 4♠.

(e) Only 7 HCP, but a decent 6-card holding in their suit. Pass. You are happy with the contract as it is. Partner may be expecting you to bid, but you, on this occasion, know better!

10
Slam Bidding

The staple fare of bidding is finding and making game contracts. One side or the other should bid game on virtually half the deals. Rarer, perhaps one deal in ten, there is the chance to bid and make a small slam, six of something.

For a small slam the partnership needs 33 points, for a grand slam 37. Do your exploring to find the right denomination first. But even on hands where you have the values to win 12 tricks there may be the possibility of two quick losers. For example, can you have 33 points and be missing two aces? Not if all those points are high-card points (there are 40 points in the pack, and two aces represent 8 of them). But where you have counted in long-suit or short-suit points then your side's high-card points add to 32 or less and you may be missing two aces.

This was a regular problem in the early days of contract bridge. In 1933 American Easley Blackwood came up with a solution that has proved highly popular. His idea was to use an artificial call for one partner to ask the other how many aces he held, with artificial responses to show no ace, one ace etc. The enquirer would then know the total number of aces the partnership held, and by subtracting from four, work out the number of aces held by the opponents.

Blackwood had to decide what bid to use as asking for aces. The snag with all conventions is that you cannot have a bid both as natural and as artificial, so he hit on the idea of using 4NT, a bid rarely needed as a natural contract (3NT is the game call), as the artificial bid. The ace-asking convention is not normally used where just high-card points are relevant, so the auctions 1NT – 4NT, and 2NT – 4NT remain as natural invitations to 6NT, accepted when opener is maximum in HCP. But in auctions where the partnership has agreed either directly, or by inference, on a trump suit, the bid of 4NT is used to mean 'How many aces have you got, partner?' The replies are:

with:	no aces:	5♣
	one ace:	5♢
	two aces:	5♡
	three aces:	5♠

A response to show four aces is not really needed, as partner is not likely to be asking with none, but the technically correct answer is an 'impossible' 5♣. The enquirer momentarily panics thinking the side, with no aces between the two of them, is already two levels too high, then realises, hopefully, the response must show four rather than none.

Here is an example of the use of *Blackwood*, with West as dealer and the opponents silent:

West	East
♠ K Q J	♠ 2
♡ 9 8 4 2	♡ A K Q 10 7 3
◇ Q J 10 3 2	◇ K 4
♣ K	♣ A Q 3 2

West	East
West	**East**
1◇	2♡
3♡	4NT
5♣	5♡
Pass	

West with 12 HCP and 1 long-suit point, opens 1◇. East, with 18 HCP and 2 long-suit points, makes the jump shift of 2♡ (16+). The partnership is in a game-forcing auction, so West's raise to 3♡ is not a limit bid. It just confirms the partnership has located the trump suit. East can now be sure the side has 33+ points but some of these are shape points, so checks up on aces. West's response shows none, so East 'signs off' in 5♡.

If West's hand had been:

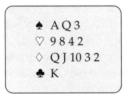

♠ A Q 3
♡ 9 8 4 2
◇ Q J 10 3 2
♣ K

the bidding would start the same way, but West's response to 4NT would be 5◇, showing one ace, and East would happily bid 6♡.

And if West had held:

♠ A K
♡ 9 8 4 2
◇ A J 7 3 2
♣ K 5

the bidding would again start the same way, but West's response to 4NT would be 5♡, showing two aces. East now knows the side has all the aces, and possibly enough for a grand slam, and can use the extension to the Blackwood convention, a bid of 5NT to ask for kings. West responds 6♡ to show both missing kings and East, being able to count all 13 tricks, bids 7NT.

Blackwood is a very popular convention even with quite inexperienced players, so some words of warning. First, it is not so much intended as a means of bidding slams, but rather as a means of keeping out of slams where you have the values but not the requisite number of aces. Second, it does not work well when clubs are trumps as the responses may commit the side to slam when two aces are missing. Enquirer will need to have at least two aces to be in safe territory when responder has only one. Third, Blackwood does not cope well with deals where it matters which rather than how many aces partner has. For example, if one player has a side suit with a no cards in it, a void, then it may matter whether one of partner's aces is in that suit (and therefore wasted) or elsewhere. Similarly if there is a danger the side has two quick losers in one suit then Blackwood will not provide a solution when an ace is missing, as you will fear two quick losers in the one suit, and you cannot ask about kings without committing the partnership to slam. Indeed the Blackwood call of 5NT after 4NT normally means enquirer knows all the aces are present and is thinking of a grand slam.

Having located a good trump suit and the necessary values for a slam the crucial thing becomes your 'control' of the side suits. An ace or a void is called 'first-round control' because you can win the first round of the suit if it is led by an opponent. A king or a singleton is called a 'second-round control' because you cannot win the trick if an opponent leads an ace, but can win the next round if the suit is continued. Provided you have either the ace, or second-round control of every side suit (as East did in the previous example), then Blackwood will tell you how many quick tricks you are missing.

But there are many deals where Blackwood will not solve the problem, so expert players have other ways of checking whether slam is sound. The most important of these is called *cue-bidding*. The essence here is that a player shows which aces, rather than how many he holds. For example consider this auction, with no opposition bidding: 1♠ – 4♠ – 5♣.

What can the 5♣ bid mean? It cannot be a suggestion that clubs be trumps, as obviously spades are agreed. Is the bidder interested in slam? Clearly, yes, as otherwise he would have Passed 4♠. So the bid is used to mean 'I am interested in slam but have a hand where it is which aces you hold, rather than how many, that will decide whether we bid it. Don't worry about the club suit, but tell me whether you hold the ace of diamonds or the ace of hearts by bidding that suit. If you have neither of these, sign-off in 5♠.' Opener may have a hand like this:

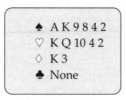

```
♠ A K 9 8 4 2
♡ K Q 10 4 2
◊ K 3
♣ None
```

If the auction starts 1♠ – 4♠, opener should reckon a slam is on if partner
has one of the red aces. You should be able to visualise this without
relying on point count. Partner has at least 4-card support in spades, so
with ten spades between you there should be no losers in the suit and the
opponents' trumps can be drawn in two rounds (three missing spades
normally divide 2-1). If partner has the ace of hearts you will be able to
trump any losing hearts, and at worst will have to lead towards the king
of diamonds for a twelfth trick. If partner has the ace of diamonds, you
will have no losing diamonds, and at worst will have to play the heart
suit for one loser.

   If you are relying on point count then in addition to 15 HCP and 3
long-suit points the hand now has 4 short-suit points, i.e. a total of 22.
Partner is in the range 13-15, so clearly the side has the values for a slam.
However, if you ask for aces and responder shows one you will not know
what to do next. His ace might be the ace of clubs, with the opponents'
having both red aces to cash. Or his ace might be a red ace, in which case
the opponents' ace of clubs will do them no good as you can trump it.
You need to know which ace partner has.

   To locate this over 4♠ you bid 5♣, a *cue-bid*. Partner will either cue-
bid a red ace or, without either, return to 5♠. Note there is no such thing
as cue-bidding in the trump suit, a bid of the trump suit is always used
to mean: 'I have nothing more to show without committing the side to
what may be too high a level.' If partner bids 5♠ over 5♣ you must
assume both red aces are missing and Pass.

   By contrast, if partner does hold a red ace, he will cue-bid, and
should show the lowest red ace he has. By lowest, we mean the first
available to show of the diamond ace and the heart ace. Suppose he bids
5♡ over 5♣. You now know he has the ace of hearts but does not have the
ace of diamonds. So you should bid 6♠. If over 5♣, partner had bid 5◊,
you would know he had the ace of diamonds, but would not know
whether he held the ace of hearts. Of course, if you 'signed off' in 5♠,
partner, with both red aces, should move on anyway as he controls both
the side suits that you don't. But over 5◊ you should actually be thinking
of a grand slam if he holds both red aces. The solution is for you to bid
6♣! Having already shown you the ace of diamonds, he will now cue-bid

the ace of hearts if he has it, and you can jump to 7♠. If he does not hold the ace of hearts he must sign off in 6♠ (you did not cue-bid 5♡ over 5◊ so he knows that ace is missing).

That illustration of cue-bidding was at the Five level, but look at this auction with opponents silent: 1♠ – 3♠ – 4◊.

Spades are agreed as trumps, and the partnership is now committed to game, so the 4◊ bid must show interest in slam. It is a cue-bid. As the bidder makes the first cue-bid possible, the bid means not only 'I control diamonds', it also means: 'I don't have the ace of clubs.' Partner must cue-bid the ace of hearts if he has it. Without the ace of hearts or clubs, partner must return to 4♠. The awkward situation is where partner has the ace of clubs but not the ace of hearts. To show the ace of clubs he will have to go to a higher level. In general he should do so, for that may be the strong hand's only worry. Suppose you hold as dealer:

♠ A K 9 8 4 2
♡ None
◊ A K J 3 2
♣ 9 4

With 15 HCP and 3 long-suit points, you open 1♠. Partner raises to 3♠, showing 10-12 points with at least four spades. You upgrade your hand by 4 short-suit points making slam within sight. Blackwood will not help if partner proves to hold only one ace. If you are missing the ace of clubs, you might also be missing the king, and you have two losers whatever partner has in hearts. The solution after the response of 3♠ is to cue-bid 4◊.

If partner has neither the heart ace nor club ace, he will sign off in 4♠, and you Pass. If partner has the heart ace he will cue-bid '4♡'. You return to 4♠ and now it is clear it was the clubs you were worried about. If he also has the ace of clubs he will move on, cue-bidding it at the five level. Where partner has the ace of clubs but not the ace of hearts, he may be in doubt whether to risk going to 5♣, but should normally do so. For example, his hand might be:

♠ Q 7 5 3
♡ Q 8 4 3
◊ 10 7
♣ A Q 3

He has 10 HCP and when you opened 1♠, one short-suit point = 11. He raised to 3♠. When you cue-bid 4◇ his hand does not look wonderful for a slam, but if he summons up a 5♣ cue-bid, the side will reach 6♠ and the slam will be odds on. Even if the club finesse fails you should be able to trump any losing diamonds in dummy.

Slam bidding is not easy. The key cards that convert a slam into a good proposition may be hard to locate. Suppose in the previous example, we change responder's red queens so the hands become:

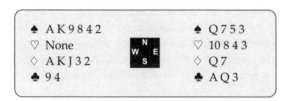

```
♠ A K 9 8 4 2        ♠ Q 7 5 3
♡ None         N     ♡ 10 8 4 3
◇ A K J 3 2   W   E  ◇ Q 7
♣ 9 4          S     ♣ A Q 3
```

Now 7♠ is a good contract as you expect to be able to draw trumps, cash all the diamonds throwing away dummy's losing clubs, and trump your second club! But even the experts will find that one hard to reach.

Summary of Slam Bidding

- You need 33 points for a small slam, 37 for a grand. Always do the exploring first to find the right denomination. When you have located a good trump fit and the necessary values for 12 winners, you still need to consider whether you may be missing two quick tricks that the opponents may cash before you get the lead. Think about your 'controls' in each of the three side suits.

- Where you have the ace or second round control of every side suit, but may be missing two aces (or one if you are thinking of a grand slam), then use Blackwood to check up on how many aces partner has. If clubs are trumps you will need to have two aces yourself, or partner's response of 5◊ would be embarrassing.

- Where you have a void, or a side suit with two quick losers, or clubs are trumps and you have only one ace, then Blackwood will not solve your problem. Consider using cue-bidding. To cue-bid, both players must know what the trump suit is, and the side must be committed to game or higher. Cue-bid the lowest first round control you have in a side suit. If partner has first round control of a side suit that he can show without increasing the level of the final contract, he must cue-bid that suit. If he has no side-suit control to show he must return to the trump suit. If he has a control to show but this takes the bidding to a higher level then he must judge whether the extra risk is justified by the chance of reaching a good slam.

Exercises for Slam Bidding

Q1 Partner opens 1♠. What would you bid holding:

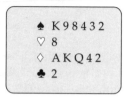

```
♠ K98432
♡ 8
♢ AKQ42
♣ 2
```

Also consider your subsequent bids.

A1 Bidding 4NT straightaway is a reasonable gamble, depending for its success only on opener having at least one ace. If opener shows no aces, bad luck! You will be in 5♠ missing three aces. But the great bulk of the time partner will respond either :

(a) 5♢ to show one ace, whereupon you sign off in 5♠, knowing it will be a sound contract, or

(b) 5♡, showing two aces, and you can bid 6♠, or

(c) 5♠, showing three aces, and you can bid 7♠.

Q2 (a) How might these hands be bid, first if West is dealer, and secondly when East is dealer:

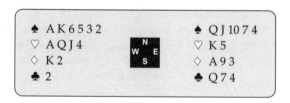

```
♠ AK6532          ♠ QJ1074
♡ AQJ4            ♡ K5
♢ K2             ♢ A93
♣ 2              ♣ Q74
```

(b) Repeat the exercise with the same West hand but with East now holding the hand in the diagram below:

```
♠ AK6532          ♠ QJ1074
♡ AQJ4            ♡ K5
♢ K2             ♢ QJ3
♣ 2              ♣ KJ4
```

A2 (a)

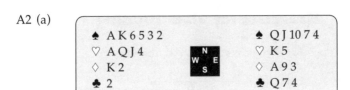

♠ A K 6 5 3 2   ♠ Q J 10 7 4
♡ A Q J 4   ♡ K 5
◇ K 2   ◇ A 9 3
♣ 2   ♣ Q 7 4

When West is the dealer with 17 HCP and 2 long-suit points, he opens 1♠. East with 4-card support for spades, 12 HCP, one long suit and one short-suit point, raises to 4♠ (13-15 with four card support). West upgrades his hand by 3 short-suit points to give him 22, and 35 for the partnership. With the ace or second round control of every side suit West bids 4NT. East responds 5◇ to show one ace. West should take a shot at 6♠ as the slam should not be worse than the heart finesse.

When East is the dealer he opens 1♠ and West may take charge at once by bidding 4NT. The auction then continues as before: 5◇ – 6♠ – Pass.

(b)

♠ A K 6 5 3 2   ♠ Q J 10 7 4
♡ A Q J 4   ♡ K 5
◇ K 2   ◇ Q J 3
♣ 2   ♣ K J 4

When West is dealer the bidding again starts 1♠ – 4♠. To West's 4NT East responds 5♣ to show no ace and West signs off in 5♠.
When East is dealer the auction will go: 1♠ – 4NT – 5♣ – 5♠ – Pass.

Q3 (a) How might these hands be bid, first if West is dealer and secondly when East is dealer:

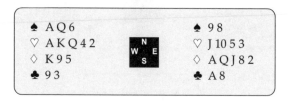

```
♠ A Q 6              ♠ 9 8
♡ A K Q 4 2          ♡ J 10 5 3
◊ K 9 5              ◊ A Q J 8 2
♣ 9 3                ♣ A 8
```

(b) Repeat the exercise with the same West hand but with East now holding the hand in the diagram below:

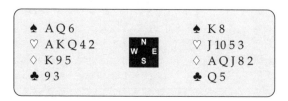

```
♠ A Q 6              ♠ K 8
♡ A K Q 4 2          ♡ J 10 5 3
◊ K 9 5              ◊ A Q J 8 2
♣ 9 3                ♣ Q 5
```

A3 (a) With West dealer, having 18 HCP, and 1 long-suit point, West opens 1♡. East with 12 HCP, 1 long-suit point, and now 2 short-suit points, raises to 4♡. West upgrades by one short suit-point, and knows the partnership has 33 points, but could have two quick losers in clubs. He moves on by cue-bidding 4♠. As this commits the side to at least 5♡, East must cue-bid 5♣. Even if West bids only 5♡, East with first round control of diamonds and a maximum hand should bid on with 6◊. West does not have enough to bid Seven, so settles for 6♡.

With East the dealer, he opens 1◊. West makes the jump shift of 2♡ (16+). East raises to 3♡. As the partnership is in a game forcing auction this is not a limit bid, East is simply saying: 'I agree hearts will be trumps and we are on our way to at least 4♡.' So now West can cue-bid 3♠. East cue-bids 4♣, and now West can safely bid 4NT as he knows the side does not have two quick losers in clubs. East bids 5♡ to show two aces, and West can try 5NT for kings. East responds 6♣ to show no kings and West settles for 6♡.
The impressive auction has been:

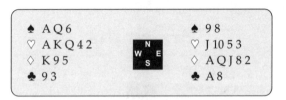

	♠ A Q 6		♠ 9 8
	♡ A K Q 4 2		♡ J 10 5 3
	◇ K 9 5		◇ A Q J 8 2
	♣ 9 3		♣ A 8

West	East
	1◇
2♡	3♡
3♠	4♣
4NT	5♡
5NT	6♣
6♡	Pass

(b)

	♠ A Q 6		♠ K 8
	♡ A K Q 4 2		♡ J 10 5 3
	◇ K 9 5		◇ A Q J 8 2
	♣ 9 3		♣ Q 5

When East has no club control the auctions begin the same way but
when West cue-bids spades, East will cue-bid diamonds. West, not
hearing of a club control, signs off in hearts at the lowest possible
level.

West	East
	1◇
2♡	3♡
3♠	4◇
4♡	Pass

11
Pre-empts

As the opening bids at the two level, including the unlimited-strength 2♣, cover all hands too powerful to open at the one level, what does an opening bid at the three level mean? Opportunities to explore for a trump suit by either side have been greatly curtailed, so it is universal practice to use these openings as obstructive bids on weak hands with very long suits, at least seven cards. The correct strength for an opening Three bid in any suit is 6-9 HCP and a decent seven card suit. Something like this:

```
♠ 3
♡ K Q J 9 7 3 2
◇ Q 3 2
♣ 8 4
```

Open 3♡. Note that if you had 10 HCP and a seven card suit (worth 3 long-suit points) you would have a total of 13 points and be too strong to open 3♡. Instead you would open with a normal exploratory 1♡ and then keep on repeating the hearts to show the extra length.

You might be thinking, 'What if partner has a poor hand? Aren't you far too high?'

Suppose for a moment partner has only six points. You will fail in your contract, but don't worry. If your side has only 14 HCP the opponents have 26 and a game contract somewhere. Depending on their vulnerability left to their own devices you can expect them to score up 420 or 620 in, say, 4♠. That means you are writing down –420 or –620. If you are actually fare better than this by scoring, say, –300, you should be happy. And even –500 is no disaster. Many teachers make that the test for whether you can risk opening at the three level. They say: 'Imagine the opponents are unkind enough to double and partner puts down a rubbishy hand; if you don't expect to lose more than 500 the risk is acceptable.'

However, if you actually observe experts bidding you will find many of them taking bigger risks than that, merely because of the great problems the high level opening gives to opponents. Non-vulnerable open this hand 3♠:

```
♠ Q J 10 8 7 3 2
♡ 3
◇ K 9 3
♣ 8 4
```

If things go badly for you the penalty might well be 800, but on some of those occasions the opponents will be able to make a slam. On a good day both opponents, having only 13 points each, might decide not to risk entering the auction and you have scored a great coup, maybe –100 for a couple off undoubled, instead of the –620 you would have scored had you left them to bid and make 4♡. The French word for pre-empt is *barrage*, very descriptive. Your opening at a high level has raised a barrage against the opponents exploring. They have to gamble. If they enter the auction and find your partner with a good hand they are in big trouble. If they timidly Pass they may miss a great contract their way.

The most effective moment to pre-empt is as dealer. The opponents know nothing about their partner's hand. If your right-hand opponent *(RHO)* has Passed, to pre-empt in second or third seat is also fine, but your left-hand opponent at least knows his partner has less than an opening bid. To pre-empt in fourth seat is pointless unless you actually expect to make your contract.

Can you pre-empt once the other side has opened? Yes, but your left-hand opponent has the extra information provided by his partner's opening, and therefore will make the winning decision more often against you.

What level defines an overcall as a pre-empt? The answer in the Acol system is that it is NOT the level at which you bid, but the number of levels you have missed out that is the key.

Suppose you are second to speak and dealer has opened 1♡. If you overcall 1♠ that will be the normal exploratory overcall (9-16 points and at least five spades). If you overcall 2♠, i.e. you have missed out one level, that is strong (something like six or seven playing tricks and at least six spades). But if you jump to 3♠, missing out two levels then that is a pre-empt, a weak hand with at least seven spades.

Now suppose your long suit is clubs. Again dealer opens 1♡. Now 2♣ is the normal overcall (12+ points and at least five clubs), 3♣ becomes the strong bid and to pre-empt you would have to bid 4♣. So, it is not the level at which you bid, but the number of levels you miss out that is the crucial matter. That is the official Acol definition of a pre-empt, but these days many experts believe jump overcalls should not be strong. With a strong overcall they either make a heavy-weight simple overcall or start with a take-out double, leaving any jump overcall as a pre-empt (though, at the two level, you would only need a 6-card suit). With any new partner that would be an area you would have to discuss before play began. 'How strong are your jump overcalls?' would be the question to ask.

Can you pre-empt when it is your partner who has opened? In official Acol the answer is yes, using the same rule as before, namely the number of levels missed out. If partner opened 1♡, the response of 1♠ is the normal exploratory bid (6-15 points with at least four spades), a 2♠ response is the jump-shift (16+), and 3♠ is the pre-empt (weak hand with at least seven spades). However, again the modern view is that pre-empting when it is only your side that has bid is far less useful than using such jumps to investigate slams. The Acol system has a particular weak spot, namely that all raises are limit bids. If you have a strong raise you lose much space needed to investigate a slam and convey only your point count.

For this reason, most players use the double-jump shifts such as 1♡ – 3♠ (where two levels have been missed out) to show a strong heart raise and slam interest. The most popular meaning would be: 'I have a raise to at least 4♡ and I have a singleton or void spade.' This method of investigating slams, for obscure reasons, is called a *splinter*. You could not play such a method without discussing it with partner. Even when using splinters note that 1♠ – 3♡, where only one level of bidding has been missed out, remains as a jump-shift showing 16+ points and hearts as your longest suit. You can see why it is essential for both partners to remember what conventions they are using if major mishaps are to be avoided.

How should you compete when it the opponent who has made a pre-empt? Making the right choice is very difficult, even for experts. That is why your opponent pre-empted. The first point to make is that you need courage, and some willingness to suffer disaster should you enter the auction and find the missing high cards lie with your lefthand opponent *(LHO)* rather than partner.

For example, suppose you hold this hand second to speak, after dealer opens 3♡:

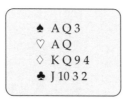

```
♠ A Q 3
♡ A Q
♢ K Q 9 4
♣ J 10 3 2
```

You are nowhere near guaranteeing a contract of 3NT on your hand alone, but with a balanced hand of 18 HCP and a double-stop in their suit, you must bid it. Look at it this way. You have 18 points, opener has perhaps 6, leaving 16 for the other two players. On average partner will have 8 points, enough for you to make 3NT in comfort, but not enough for him to make any bid on his own. So you must be the one who bids it. Of course, if LHO proves to have most of the missing points you will be in big trouble, but, in the long run, you will score worse by Passing.

Now suppose you hold:

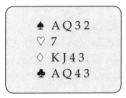

♠ A Q 3 2
♡ 7
◇ K J 4 3
♣ A Q 4 3

Dealer, to your right, opens 3♡. You certainly must bid, and to overcall on a 4-card suit would be asking for trouble. For this reason virtually all experts use a Double of a pre-empt as take-out, just as they would had the opening been 1♡ (but with a slighter better hand than that promised at the one level). You are saying: 'I have the points to justify bidding, but you, partner, must select the trump suit.' With anything up to about 8 points partner will simply bid his longest suit at the lowest level (or 3NT with values in their suit). He can more readily Pass the take-out double for penalties than he would at the one level because opener has to make nine tricks to succeed, and has fewer points than normal. But for partner to Pass the take-out double he must have length in their suit. If the opponents have, say, ten hearts between them, they may get close to making 3♡ even with very few high-card points.

Overcalls in a suit at three level might still be only five, but are normally 6-card suits, with better than a minimum opening bid. Partner will make a forward move with more than 8 points.

Summary for Pre-empts

- Pre-empts show a decent 7-card suit and 6-9 HCP. When no-one else has bid the pre-empt is at the three level. If RHO has opened it is the number of levels missed out that determine whether you are pre-empting. If you make a minimum call in a new suit over a one level opening, that is always the normal exploratory bid though it may have to be at the two level if your suit is junior to the one opened by the opponent. In standard Acol if you make a jump overcall missing out one level, that is a strong bid, and you must bid higher than that to pre-empt. However, many players use any jump overcall as a pre-empt (promising only six cards if at the two level) and you should discuss this matter with any new partner.

- The same rules apply in Standard Acol when it is partner that has opened, but most players these days, whilst retaining the single jump-shift to show a strong hand (16+), use a double jump-shift not as a pre-empt, but as showing a hand with slam interest and at least a raise to game in opener's suit.

- When an opponent pre-empts in front of you have some courage when deciding whether to enter the auction. If 10 points with partner would be enough to give you game, you must bid. An overcall of 3NT shows a balanced hand of at least 17 points with a stop in their suit. A double is for take-out and often short in their suit, with 3 or 4 cards in every other suit. An overcall in a suit should normally have six cards in the suit, but may be made with five good ones.

Exercises for Pre-empts

Q1 As dealer with nobody vulnerable, what would you call holding:

(a)	(b)	(c)	(d)
♠ 3	♠ 3	♠ 3	♠ 3
♡ KQ107632	♡ QJ107642	♡ KQJ7632	♡ KQJ97632
◊ AJ3	◊ K93	◊ AJ32	◊ K103
♣ 75	♣ 92	♣ 7	♣ 9

A1 (a) You have 10 HCP, too much for a pre-empt at the three level. Open 1♡.
(b) A normal 3♡ opening.
(c) Much too strong for 3♡. You must either open 1♡, or, probably better, 4♡.
(d) This time, with eight hearts, the opening is clearly 4♡.

♠ ♡ ◊ ♣

Q2 With neither side vulnerable you hold, second to speak:

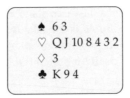

```
♠ 63
♡ QJ108432
◊ 3
♣ K94
```

What would you call if the dealer opened (a) 1◊, or (b) 1♠?

A2. Over 1◊ you have a clear 3♡ pre-empt. Over 1♠ it is much more difficult. In Standard Acol 3♡ would be strong so your choice is between Pass and 4♡, probably Pass. You would be better placed if you had agreed with partner that all jump overcalls were pre-empts, in which case you could make the same 3♡ call as over 1◊.

♠ ♡ ◊ ♣

Q3 With neither side vulnerable you are next to speak after the dealer opens 3♡. What would you call holding:

(a)	(b)	(c)	(d)
♠ K J 10 5	♠ 6 5	♠ K J 10 9 3	♠ A 9
♡ 6 5	♡ K J 10 5	♡ 6	♡ A Q
◇ A Q 6	◇ A J 6	◇ A J 5 3 2	◇ K Q J 3 2
♣ A J 4 2	♣ A 9 4 2	♣ A 9	♣ J 10 4 2

A3 (a) Double (for take-out)

(b) Pass. Too weak to bid 3NT. 3♡ will probably fail but you cannot double as that would be for take-out promising support in the other suits (something you conspicuously lack in spades). Of course after you Pass, if your partner makes a take-out double you will have the luxury between choosing to bid 3NT or Passing (knowing they are going off in 3♡ doubled).

(c) 3♠. Only 13 HCP and only five spades, but there are 2 long-suit points, a decent shape and solid looking spades, so the overcall is sound.

(d) 3NT. You have 17 HCP, a balanced hand, and a double stop in their suit. Perfect! You must not double with only two spades, and you must not overcall 4◇ cutting out the most likely game.

12

More Advanced Auctions

As you come across more sequences you will see some where logic dictates a modification of the rules learned so far. Consider this sequence:

West	East
1♡	2♣
2NT	3♡

East's 3♡ is delayed support for opener, showing three cards in the heart suit. But it is not a limit bid, as you have might have expected from earlier rules, for a sound reason. West's rebid of 2NT did not deny holding five hearts, so East does not know whether West has four or five hearts. So, if East has three, he wants to give West a choice between 3NT and 4♡ as the game to be in. He can only do this by showing his 3-card support en route to game. If West has only four hearts he must return to 3NT, so if he has five he must go on to 4♡. West must not Pass 3♡.

So far the artificial bids covered have been:
  (a) The negative response of 2NT to an opening bid of 2♠, 2♡ or 2◇;
  (b) The opening 2♣ (meaning 23/24 balanced, or a game going hand of any shape) and its negative response of 2◇;
  (c) The take-out double over an opening one or three of a suit (meaning 'I have enough points to justify bidding, you choose the trump suit')
  (d) The Blackwood 4NT asking for aces and its responses, its extension of 5NT for kings, and some other, more advanced, methods of investigating slams such as cue-bidding or splinters.

There are three other artificial bids with which all players should be familiar.

1 Bidding the opponent's suit

Look at the following auction:

West	North	East	South
1♡	1♠	2♠	

What can 2♠ mean? It would be pointless for East to suggest spades as trumps when North has overcalled in the suit promising five, particularly as if East doubled it would be for penalties, meaning: 'I don't think they can make 1♠.' In Standard Acol the bid of an opponent's suit is used to mean, 'We have enough values to make a game contract, let's keep exploring until we find the right denomination.'

The idea would be particularly useful in this sort of situation:

West	North	East	South
1◊	Dbl	Pass	?

West has opened 1◊, North has made a take-out double (showing 13+ points and 3 or 4 cards in all the suits other than diamonds) and East has Passed. What should South bid, holding:

```
♠ A Q 3 2
♡ K J 8 4
◊ 4 3
♣ A 8 3
```

South has enough to bid a game but which one? You don't want to gamble on 4♡ or 4♠ without being sure partner has 4-card support, and you recall that all new suit bids in response to a take-out double are limit bids, i.e. it is wrong to bid 2♡ or 2♠: partner would Pass with a minimum hand.

The solution is to bid 2◊, the opponent's suit. Note this does not show diamonds. If you had reasonable diamonds you would bid no-trumps; if you had very long diamonds you would Pass 1◊ doubled. You can never want to bid 2◊ in its natural sense of wishing to play in that contract. So it is ideal to have the understanding that it means: 'We have enough for game, keep exploring.' Over 2◊, partner will show his 4-card major and you will raise him to game in that suit, knowing you have eight trumps between you.

---

2 *Fourth suit forcing*

Consider this auction:

West	North	East	South
1♢	Pass	1♡	Pass
2♣	Pass	2♠	

Can West have four spades? No, because he would have shown the suit by rebidding 1♠ over 1♡ rather than 2♣. So there is little point in East suggesting spades as trumps. It would be more natural for East to bid no-trumps when he has the majors whilst partner has the minors. So that bid of 2♠ by East is rarely needed in its natural meaning of 'I have four spades.'

However, suppose East held:

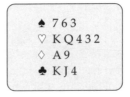

♠ 7 6 3
♡ K Q 4 3 2
♢ A 9
♣ K J 4

The auction has begun 1♢ – 1♡ – 2♣. What should East bid on the second round?

He has the values for a game contract but to repeat the hearts would be a limit bid, and he certainly does not want to jump to 4♡ not knowing of any support opposite. The solution is to use the fourth suit, 2♠, as a mechanism for saying, 'Let's continue exploring, but don't assume I have four spades'

If West held:

♠ 9
♡ J 10 4
♢ K Q 10 4 2
♣ A Q 7 2

his clear-cut continuation would be 3♡, showing 3-card support (remember he has denied 4-card support when he did not raise the heart response straight away) and responder could choose 4♡ as the game. By contrast, if West held:

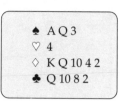

```
♠ A Q 3
♡ 4
◇ K Q 10 4 2
♣ Q 10 8 2
```

His continuation after 1◇ – 1♡ – 2♣ – 2♠ would be 2NT and East would choose 3NT as the game contract.

Of course, had the auction been:

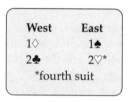

West	East
1◇	1♠
2♣	2♡*
*fourth suit	

it is quite possible BOTH players have four hearts. West's shape might be 0-4-5-4 meaning he has no spades, four hearts, five diamonds, and four clubs and East might hold five spades and four hearts. But the bid of the fourth suit retains the meaning: 'Let's explore, but don't assume I have four cards in the fourth suit.' If West has four hearts he can raise to 3♡. East will then either go on to 4♡ if he has four, or retire to 3NT if he was looking for something in hearts.

3 The Stayman Convention

Chapter 7 covered the opening 1NT and responses. This was the scheme of responses:

Responses to the Opening 1NT			
Is there a game on? Responder's hand	NO (0-10)	MAYBE (11-12)	YES (13+)
Balanced shape	Pass	2NT	3NT
6-card suit (e.g. spades)	2♠		4♠
5-card suit (e.g. spades)	2♠		3♠
4-card suit (e.g. spades)	Pass		

There are some gaps to be filled. Suppose partner has opened 1NT and you have game-values with a 4-card major, such as:

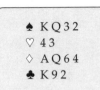

```
        ♠ K Q 3 2
        ♡ 4 3
        ◇ A Q 6 4
        ♣ K 9 2
```

You cannot show your 4-card spade suit. 2♠ would be the weakness take-out and 3♠ would be the jump-shift promising five so partner raises with 3-card support.

At the moment you would have to raise to 3NT. This would probably be the right contract unless opener held four spades with you. In that case 4♠ is likely to be a safer contract than 3NT. True you have to make ten tricks rather than nine, but the extra trick is usually made after drawing trumps in three rounds by making the last two trumps separately by ruffing a loser. Furthermore if your side has eight spades, it is more likely you have a weak spot elsewhere (probably hearts on this occasion). If the opponent on lead strikes at your weak spot on his opening lead against 3NT, they may well establish winners in the suit to cash when they next regain the lead. The benefit of a trump suit could avoid this danger.

During the Second World War one of the inventors of the Acol system, Jack Marx, came up with a solution to this problem but as Bridge Magazine ceased publication during the war, his ideas did not appear in the publication until 1946. Meanwhile in America, George Rapee had had the same idea, written up by journalist Sam Stayman in the American Bridge magazine of June 1945. It was Stayman's name that became linked to the convention. This was that responder, instead of telling opener of his major suit, should ask opener whether he held a major. The bid to ask this question was 2♣ and opener would respond:

> 2♡: 'I have four cards in the heart suit'
> 2♠: 'I have four cards in the spade suit'
> 2◇: 'I do not have four cards in either hearts or spades'

Where opener has four cards in both majors most people will bid the lowest, hearts, first but in reality, for reasons that will become clear in a moment, it does not matter much if you choose to bid the better one.

Look at the hand shown above. East has 14 HCP and four spades. His partner opens 1NT. If they have agreed to use the Stayman convention East can respond 2♣ to enquire whether West has a 4-card major. If West responds 2♠ East raises to 4♠. If West responds 2◇ or 2♡ East's next bid is 3NT. He sought a fit in spades and did not find it. Suppose now West had both majors. He showed hearts first, and East chose 3NT. Yet East had asked about a major suit. Clearly East has the other one, spades, and West can choose 4♠ as the final contract.

Now suppose East has only an invitational hand of 11 points with four spades:

```
    ♠ K Q 3 2
    ♡ 4 3
    ◇ A Q 6 4
    ♣ 10 8 3
```

East needs to know two things about opener's hand:

(a) Does West have four spades?
(b) Is West's strength at the lower or upper end of his possible range?

To find the answer to both these questions East uses the Stayman convention, and responds 2♣. If West bids 2♠, East will raise to 3♠, showing the partnership has found its 4-4 fit in spades, but leaving opener the final decision of whether to go on to 4♠.

If West bids 2♡ or 2◇ (no major), East must next bid 2NT, saying: 'We have not found a fit, but you can go on to 3NT if you are in the upper range for your opening 1NT.' Actually West has four sensible bids he can make:

(a) Pass with lower range and not 4 spades;
(b) Raise to 3NT with upper range and not 4 spades;
(c) Move to 3♠ if he has lower range and both majors (having shown the hearts first, which East did not like, he knows East must have spades);
(d) Bid 4♠ with upper range and both majors.

Next let us tackle the thorny problem of responding to 1NT holding a 5- or 6-card major with an invitational-strength hand. A bid of the major at the two level would be a weakness take-out and end the auction, a jump-shift would be game-forcing. The somewhat unsatisfactory solution using Stayman in official Acol is to enquire about opener's majors, but ignore the answer, and then bid your suit at the three level. For example:

West	East
1NT	2♣
2♠ (or 2◇)	3♡

In standard Acol this 3♡ bid shows 5 or 6 hearts, invitational. West can Pass, return to 3NT, or raise to 4♡. The snag is that with only two hearts and a lower range strength he either has to Pass what may be a 7-card fit, or go to 3NT with insufficient points. This problem can be solved by using 'Transfer Bids' a convention outside the scope of this book.

Stayman has the same snag as all conventions, namely you cannot have both the natural meaning (weakness take-out into 2♣) and the artificial meaning ('Have you got a 4-card major, partner?'). So what does responder do when he actually has long clubs? In standard Acol the jump shift of 3♣ remains strong, offering opener the option of returning to 3NT if he does not like clubs, or supporting the suit if he does. The only invitational raise is 2NT and this should be used even with a long minor as the 11 tricks needed for game in a minor will be out of reach.

And when you have a weakness take-out into clubs? Then you bid 2♣ (which partner takes as Stayman) and continue with 3♣ to play, i.e. 'I wish we were not playing Stayman! I wanted to stop in 2♣.' As you are committed to 3♣ only make this take-out with six clubs. Holding only five clubs and a weak hand Pass the opening 1NT.

Can Stayman be used on any other hand not interested in game? Not as originally intended but bridge players soon thought of an occasion. Suppose you hold this terrible hand:

```
        ♠ J 9 6 3
        ♡ Q 8 7 2
        ◇ 10 9 5 3 2
        ♣ None
```

Partner opens 1NT. What do you do? Your first reaction may be panic. Partner has a minimum opening hand and we have only 3 HCP. We are too high already. Your second, more helpful idea is to make the weakness take-out into diamonds, which will probably be a better contract than 1NT. But, using Stayman, there is a better solution. Respond 2♣! Provided partner remembers this is asking for a 4-card major, he will either bid one, in which case you happily Pass, or he will bid 2◇, in which case again you Pass and are no worse off than before. Indeed you are better off, as partner is declarer. You can put down your lousy dummy and offer to get partner a drink from the bar.

Only you knew you were intending to Pass any response from opener. You have quite legitimately put Stayman to a use for which it was not originally designed.

Here is the extended table of responses to the opening 1NT using Stayman:

Responses to the Opening 1NT using Stayman			
Is there a game on?	NO (0-10)	MAYBE (11-12)	YES (13+)
Responder's hand			
Balanced shape	Pass	2NT	3NT
6-card suit (e.g. spades)	2♠	2♣ then 3♠	4♠
5-card suit (e.g. spades)	2♠	2♣ then 3♠	3♠
4-card suit (e.g. spades)	Pass	2♣ then raise to 3♠ or 2NT	2♣ then raise to 4♠ or 3NT
Long clubs (5 or 6)	2♣ then 3♣	2NT	3♣

The Stayman convention can also be used after an opening bid of 2NT, when the response of 3♣ asks opener to bid a major suit he holds.

You may be wondering whether there is any end to these conventions. In theory, no. When beginners first learn bridge they often have a mental picture that there is a fixed box of knowledge to absorb, and that when the lessons are complete they will have covered it all. On learning their first convention they begin to sense that the box is unlimited in size. Bidding theory has continued to evolve since contract bridge began.

Fortunately the basic principles of bidding covered by this book will allow you to cope with the great majority of problems you come across. But if you want to add icing to the cake there is much more to learn.

By contrast this book has only touched upon the basic principles of play and defence. There is a lifetime of learning ahead. Counting your tricks, planning the play, handling entries, combining chances, endplays, safety plays, squeezes. These are some of the techniques you might acquire. If the list was not almost endless, the addicts or professionals, playing more than a hundred deals a week for most weeks of the year would soon be bored. They do not, for every new deal presents a new set of problems and you will never come across the same deal twice.

Summary for More Advanced Auctions

- The logic of some auctions will allow you to realise that they are forcing rather than limit bids. For example in the auction 1♡ – 2♣ – 2NT – 3♡ the last bid must be forcing as East cannot know whether West has four or five hearts and is offering a choice between 3NT and 4♡ as the game contracts.

- Bidding the suit proposed by the opponent's as trumps is rarely a natural bid. The normal meaning is: 'We have enough values to bid game, let's explore until we reach a game contract.' It is used as a means both for showing strength and for continuing exploration when no natural bid is available that would describe the hand well.

- When someone bids the fourth suit (i.e. all the other three have been suggested as trumps by the same side) it does not promise four cards in the suit, but is simply a means of continuing exploration. It implies the bidder has no natural, limit bid available that would describe his hand.

- The response of 2♣ to an opening 1NT is usually agreed by partners to be the convention known as Stayman. This asks opener for a 4-card major. Opener either bids a major in which he has four cards or, if he does not have four cards in either major he bids 2◊. The convention is used to locate a 4-4 fit in a major suit to select that as the denomination in preference to 2NT or 3NT.

Exercises for More Advanced Auctions

Q1 West holds as dealer:

♠ K Q 3
♡ K Q 6 3
◊ 10 7 2
♣ A K 2

West with a balanced hand of 17 HCP is too strong for 1NT and too weak for 2NT, so opens 1♡. East responds 1♠ and now West jumps to 2NT showing 17-18 HCP in a balanced hand. East now continues by bidding 3♡. What should West do?

A1 East's bid of 3♡ shows delayed support of three cards for West's opening (where West might still hold five, despite rebidding 2NT to show 17 points, balanced), and it is forcing, not a limit bid. West must return the compliment by bidding 3♠, denying five hearts but showing three-card support for East's spades where East still might have five. If East has only four spades he will not Pass but return to 3NT. The bids of 3♡ and 3♠ are forcing because they are the only way to locate a 5-3 fit in either major. If there is no 8-card fit you end in 3NT, so if you find one, it is only sensible to proceed to game in the major.

Q2 East holds, third to speak:

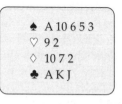

♠ A 10 6 5 3
♡ 9 2
◊ 10 7 2
♣ A K J

West opens 1♡, East responds 1♠ and West rebids 2♣. What should East bid now?

A2 East has 12 HCP and 1 long-suit point and West has opened the bidding, so the partnership should be on the way to game. But which game? East wants to be in 3NT if West has values in diamonds, or 4♠ if West has 3-card support for spades. To repeat the spades would be a limit bid, so the values suggest 4♠, whilst the spade suit is not nearly good enough, given that West has not shown any support. The solution is for East to bid 2◊ the fourth suit, not promising four diamonds, but requesting that the exploration continue. If West bids 2NT, East raises to 3NT; if West shows 3-card spade support (implying short diamonds), East chooses 4♠ as the game.

Q3 East is responding to West's opening of 1NT (12-14 HCP). How should East plan the auction holding:

(a)	(b)	(c)
♠ A K 7 2	♠ A K 7 2	♠ A K 7 2
♡ 10 9 8 4 3	♡ K 10 9 4 3	♡ K 10 9 4 3
◊ 6	◊ 6	◊ 6
♣ J 9 4	♣ J 9 4	♣ A 9 4

A3 (a) East could make the weakness take-out into 2♡, but better would be to use Stayman, and respond 2♣. If West bids a major East Passes, if West bids 2◊, East removes to 2♡, showing a weak hand with five hearts (and, by inference four spades, or East would have made the weakness take-out into hearts initially).

(b) East now has an invitational hand. Again you should start with Stayman 2♣. If West shows a major, you can upgrade the hand by 2 points for the singleton diamond and raise to Four of that major. If West bids 2◊ you must jump to 3♡, non-forcing but invitational with long hearts. West can Pass, raise, or return to 3NT.

(c) East now has a game-going hand. He should jump to 3♡, game-forcing. If West has 3 card support he will go to 4♡, if he has only two hearts but four spades he can show the spades and East can raise to game. If West has only two hearts and not four spades, he will bid 3NT over 3♡.

13

Ethics and Etiquette

The media only seem to put bridge on the front page when some scandal comes to light. This gives the general public a distorted view of the game. The reality is that cheating in bridge is about as rare as it is in golf. What is much more common is ignorance of the Laws. Both for golf and bridge these are complicated because they have to be designed to cover every possible eventuality. But there are guidelines that allow players to judge in the majority of cases what good conduct is. We hope you will contact your local bridge club or teacher (Appendix B contains details), and give advice here for good conduct in a tournament.

We have stressed that bridge is a game of deduction. The Laws say what clues you are permitted to use and this is inherent to the game. The primary permitted clues are the sight of your own cards, the bids made by each player, the cards that become visible in dummy, and those revealed trick by trick. Agreements between partners before play starts about the meaning of bids made, or cards played when defending, are also permitted but suffer some restrictions in Law. They must not be secret, and are limited in number and complexity depending on the standard of event.

Let's take the matter of your agreements. You are not supposed to remind partner of them during the play of a deal, but the opponents are entitled to know them. How can this be achieved? Bridge tournaments have various mechanisms, not perfect, for solving this problem. One is a list of your agreements, a 'system card', given to your opponents so they can see what your agreements are. Another is to allow each player, when it is their turn to call or play, to ask what agreements the opponents have. However, you must treat this right with respect. Not only would it become a bore if people were constantly asking questions, but asking the question itself might reveal something about your hand. Getting the right balance here is not easy. In general the most convenient time to ask is at the end of the auction. The defender on lead may ask before leading, then select his lead and place it face downwards on the table, giving partner the chance to ask questions, and only then is the lead faced.

If an opponent asks the meaning of a particular bid by your side, it is *not* the player who made the bid who answers, but his partner. This is because the opponent is not entitled to know the hand, only the partnership agreement, so the player who cannot see the hand answers. Particularly with beginners, the hand may be very different from what it should be according to the agreement! Don't be embarrassed to reply: 'We have no agreement.' If that is the truth, it is a better answer than trying to guess. If you have read this book you will be able to reply: 'Standard Acol,' and if the bid is a convention, name it, and give further explanation if asked.

Another method used to help opponents know what is going on is the Alert procedure where the partner of the player who has made an artificial bid warns opponents that the bid is artificial, thereby giving them a chance to find out what it means when they wish to do so. When you start at a new club ask what their procedure is as practice can differ.

In terms of complexity of agreements you may take it that anything in this book is acceptable at all levels of bridge. The higher the standard event the more complexity is allowed.

Next we tackle the thorny problem of tempo of play. Bridge is a game of thought and the Laws cannot ban the process of thinking. But the process brings with it two difficulties. The first is social. Sitting around for a long time waiting for someone else to make a decision can be a bore. Players should have a feel for the tempo that is socially acceptable. For beginners this is probably the biggest hurdle they face when playing in a tournament for the first time. To a beginner every bid made and every card played may be a problem. For a more experienced player 80% of decisions may be easy, and 20% difficult. A typical time allowed for two deals is fifteen minutes. Practice meeting that target before you play in a tournament. Then you won't be embarrassed by keeping others waiting.

The second problem created by the act of thinking is that the process itself may convey information about your hand. This is not one of the clues permitted to partner. The Laws contain a bias about all mannerisms that convey information about a player's hand. They say such information can be used by an opponent (at their own risk) but not by partner. The mental knack you need here is to imagine that between you and partner there is a brick wall through which only bids made and cards played emerge. Other things such as whether partner is happy or sad, interested or bored, quick or slow to make a decision, cannot be used. For this reason it is good practice to avoid looking at partner during the bidding and play of a deal. Conversely, there is no such wall between you and an opponent and you can note any such clues you like. Unlike poker, however, it is not proper to use this fact to deceive an opponent.

When anything goes wrong, seek guidance. There is often someone present (the Tournament Director) to resolve the problem. It is the players' duty to seek a ruling if anything clear-cut has gone wrong such as a bid out of turn or a revoke (failure to follow suit when you have a card of the suit led). Where a player has inadvertently revealed something about their hand or even legitimately done so (such as by thinking for a long time) their partner is then under constraint not to take advantage, but it will be a matter of judgment what partner can do, and it is the job of the TD to make a ruling where there is an element of doubt. When you have what is called unauthorised information about your partner's hand we suggest you follow this course of action:

- Check what your reasonable actions were without this unauthorised bit of information. If there is more than one, avoid those that other people might think were prompted by the extra information. Thus you will gain a reputation for being a highly ethical player.
- If an opponent asks the TD to rule on whether the action you choose should be allowed, they are not accusing you of being unethical. They are merely saying that in such situations it is the TD's judgment of what is normal, rather than yours, that counts.

Now we turn to etiquette. Follow traditional good neighbourliness with people at your local club, saying hello as someone arrives at a table, perhaps introducing a visitor you know but the others don't.

Help the person in charge. Listen to their instructions (you may need to remember your pair number or where to sit, and when to avoid shuffling the cards!). Seek guidance with administrative tasks like scoring if you are in doubt about what to do. Keep your speed of play on schedule. Avoid chat until you have completed the deals you have to play. Don't talk about the hands noisily. A player at another table yet to play that deal may be embarrassed by overhearing what you have said.

Treat your partner as a friend! Even experienced bridge players often fail this test. If you are declarer, it is traditional to thank partner when he faces dummy. Learn to accept reverses philosophically. Many bad results are no-one's fault, or are a shared responsibility. Even when partner is at fault, what is gained by apportioning blame? Of course, if you want to apologise for an error you have made at the end of a hand that is acceptable. But criticism of partner is not. If you can help partner through a bad result not only will you both enjoy the game more, you will find you both play better. The past is over. Concentrate on the present and the future. On the next deal you must not be thinking about what went wrong on the last one.

Treat your opponents with respect. If chatting to your partner when they arrive, or after the deal, try to involve them. If you get a good result, don't gloat. Always start from the assumption that they are ethical players. If you have reason to call for a ruling always do it in a neutral tone of voice, not one that makes other players imagine a heinous crime has been committed. If it is they who call for a ruling, don't take it as a personal affront. Disputes are rare, but should they arise, help to calm the situation rather than inflate it.

Much of this advice sounds like common sense, and it is. This is an area where beginners can often show better behaviour than those who have been playing for years. Set the right tone and you will make the game pleasant for everyone.

You can enjoy golf without having a single-figure handicap, and the same applies to bridge. Once the basics are learned, bridge can provide you with a lifetime of enjoyable deduction-making, problem-solving, competition, and risk-taking. Good luck and have great fun.

Glossary

Acol: The bidding system described in this book that was developed at the Acol Bridge Club in North London in the 1930s.

Advancer: The partner of the overcaller.

Auction: The phase that preceded the play of the cards, consisting of the naming of contracts (the bids), and calls such as Pass, Double, and Redouble. The auction concludes with three consecutive Passes. The final contract named in the auction becomes the contract for the play.

Bidding: Sometimes used as an alternative word to 'auction'.

Blackwood: The convention associated with Easley Blackwood whereby 4NT is used to enquire of partner how many aces he holds, with artificial responses to show how many. The follow-up of 5NT asks for kings.

Board: The container for the four separate hands of one deal. At duplicate the board is passed from table to table so a different group of players can play the same deal.

Break: The division of the unseen cards in one suit between the two concealed hands.

Cash: To win tricks that are immediately available without losing the lead.

Claim: The curtailment of play when one player shows the remaining cards in his hand and makes a statement about the number of tricks the partnership will win of the remaining tricks.

Concession: The curtailment of play when one player shows the remaining cards in his hand and makes a statement about the number of tricks the partnership will lose of the remaining tricks.

Contract: An undertaking to win at least the stated number of tricks in a particular denomination.

Convention: A bid intended as artificial, conveying a meaning unrelated to the contract named.

Cross-ruff: In a trump contract to lead a side suit from one hand and trump in the other, and then lead a new side suit from the second hand and trump in the first.

Cue-bid: The bid of a side suit to indicate the bidder has first- or second-round control of that suit.

Cut: The random choice of card from a full deck used to determine partners and the first player to deal in rubber bridge.

Deal: Either the act of distributing the cards to the four players, or the layout of the cards once the distribution is complete.

Deck: The pack of 52 cards.

Declarer: The player who has to fulfil the contract during the play.

Defender: A player on the side opposing declarer.

Denomination: The suit (or no-trump) named in the contract.

Discard: A card played by a player who has no cards of the suit led to the trick, usually meaning a non-trump card that cannot win the trick.

Double: A call that increases the penalty for failure, and the reward for success of a contract bid by the other side.

Doubleton: A holding of two cards in one suit in a bridge hand.

Drawing trumps: Leading trumps until the opponents have no trumps left.

Dummy: The hand that is placed face upwards on the table after the opening lead has been made.

Duplicate bridge: Needs more than one table in play. Each deal is played by more than one group of four players. Comparison of scores is between partnerships at different tables that held the same cards.

Exploratory bid: A bid that does not define the bidder's strength to within one trick, i.e. the bid shows a range of strength wider than 4 points. The principal purpose is to convey information about shape in order to assist the search for the trump suit.

False-card: Play a card with the deliberate intention of misleading an opponent about the layout of the remaining cards.

Finesse: An attempt to win a trick with a card that is not the highest card out by relying on the opponent who played earlier to the trick to hold the higher card.

Follow suit: The Laws specify that after the lead has been made to a trick each player must contribute one card of the same suit as the card led to the trick, if able to do so.

Forcing: A bid which by agreement with partner will not end the auction.

Forcing to game: A bid implying the partnership has sufficient values to make a game contract.

Fourth suit forcing: A convention whereby the fourth suit to be bid by one side does not promise four cards in the suit, but ensures partner makes a further bid.

Game: Any contract that will be rewarded with the game bonus if it succeeds. It is a contract worth 100 points or more, or, in rubber bridge, one that brings the cumulative value of contracts bid and made by one side to 100 points or more.

Game forcing: A bid that implies the partnership has the values for the auction to continue until at least a game contract is reached.

Grand slam: A contract to win all thirteen tricks.

Hand: The 13 cards held by one player.

HCP: High-Card Points. Ace = 4, King = 3, Queen = 2, Jack = 1.

Honour: Any ace, king, queen, jack or ten. At rubber bridge there is a scoring bonus for one player holding four or five of the trump honours in one hand. There is a scoring bonus in no-trumps for any player holding all four aces in their hand.

Invitational bid: A bid implying the partnership can achieve a contract with a higher scoring bonus if partner's hand strength is at the top end of the range he has shown so far.

Jump overcall: Any overcall at a level higher than the legal minimum in that denomination.

Jump-shift: Following a bid by partner, a jump bid in a new suit.

Lead: The first card to be played to a trick.

Level: The number of tricks named in a contract.

LHO: Left-hand opponent.

Limit bid: A bid which defines the strength of the bidders hand to within one trick (or maybe a maximum range of 4 points). All limit bids can be Passed if partner accepts the denomination, and has insufficient strength to try for the contract that will attract a higher bonus in the scoring.

Major suits: Spades or hearts, whose contracts are worth 30 points per trick named, and where game is ten tricks, i.e. 4♠ or 4♡.

MiniBridge: A form of bridge with bidding replaced by each player saying how many points they hold. The side with most points is the declaring side, the player of that side with more points is declarer. Declarer chooses the contract after seeing dummy, but then play proceeds as in normal bridge.

Minor suits: Diamonds or clubs, whose contracts are worth 20 points per trick named, and where game is 11 tricks, i.e. 5♣ or 5◊.

No-trumps: The denomination with no trump suit. All suits have equal value. The scoring for no-trump contracts is 40 for 1NT but it goes up 30 thereafter, so 2NT is worth 70. 3NT is worth 100, and is game.

Non-vulnerable: At rubber bridge a side that has not yet made a game in the current rubber, together with the scoring bonuses and penalties that will therefore apply when that side declares a contract. At duplicate bridge a side designated on the board in play as being non-vulnerable together with the associated bonuses and penalties if that side declares a contract.

Opening bid: The first bid in the auction.

Opening lead: The first card played on a deal.

Opponent: Any member of an opposing side or team.

Overcall: The first bid by the second side to bid in an auction.

Overtake: Play a card higher than the one played to the trick by partner with the intention of obtaining the lead should your side win the trick.

Overtrick: A trick made by the declaring side in excess of the number needed to fulfil the contract.

Partner: One member of the same side (partners sit facing each other).

Part-score: A contract worth less than one hundred points, that therefore carries no game bonus.

Pin: Leading a card that is not the highest out to prevent an opponent winning a trick with a lower card that he must play due to shortness in the suit.

Psyche: A bid where the bidder deliberately misrepresents his strength or shape in order to deceive.

Redouble: A call that further increases the reward for success or the penalty for failure of a contract bid by a player of the same side that has been doubled by a player of the other side.

Responder: The partner of the player who made the opening bid.

Retaining trump control: Preserving at least one trump for the purposes of regaining the lead after the lead has been lost to an opponent who has winners to play in a suit that is not trumps.

RHO: Right-hand opponent.

Rubber bridge: The type of bridge needing only one table in play. No scoring comparison is made with any other table.

Ruff: Contributing a trump to a trick where a non-trump was led.

Sacrifice: To overcall the opponents' contract with one of your own that you do not expect to make with the intention of reducing your minus score when compared with letting the other side play and make their contract.

Shape: The number of cards that a bridge hand has in each suit, usually stated with the spade suit first, then hearts, diamonds and finally clubs e.g. 5-4-3-1.

Sign-off: A bid made in the expectation that partner will Pass.

Singleton: A holding of just one card in one suit in a bridge hand.

Small slam: A contract to win at least 12 of the 13 tricks.

Splinter: A jump bid showing a singleton or void in the suit bid.

Stayman: The response of 2♣ to an opening 1NT to enquire whether opener has four cards in either major suit.

Strength: A measure of the trick-taking potential of a hand, often numeric.

System: A coherent set of bidding agreements between partners covering the bulk of bids that may arise.

Top of a sequence: An agreement, when leading from a sequence of two or more cards adjacent in rank that include an honour, to lead the highest card of the sequence. An "interior sequence" is a sequence containing an honour that has one card higher than the sequence e.g. K 10 9 x, Q 10 9 x, K J 10 x.

Top of nothing: An agreement to lead the highest card from three or more small cards.

Trump: If the final contract names a suit as trumps, then during the play a card of this suit beats any card of the other three suits.

Underlead: To lead a card in defence from a suit containing a higher winning card.

Void: A suit in which a bridge hand has no cards.

Vulnerable: At rubber bridge a side that has already made a game in the current rubber together with the increased scoring bonuses and penalties that will therefore apply when that side declares a contract. At duplicate bridge a side designated on the board in play as being vulnerable together with the associated bonuses and penalties if that side declares a contract.

Appendix A

The ritual of the deal:

1 The player who cut the highest card, let us suppose it was South, gathers up the cards and passes the deck to the opponent on his left, West.
2 West shuffles the deck, then passes it across the table to his partner, East.
3 East cuts the deck by taking an upper portion of the deck and placing this towards the dealer, South.
4 South picks up the far portion, places it on top of the nearer portion, and then starts dealing, one card at a time face downwards, going round to the left, starting with the opponent to the left, namely West.
5 Optionally, to save time later, dealer's partner may shuffle a separate deck of cards to be used on the next deal.

In bridge whenever the players have to do something in a given order, this always goes round to the left from the player who starts. A common error in dealing is for the dealer, whilst squaring up the deck, to expose sight of the bottom card. The distribution of the cards must be secret.

As there are 52 cards in the deck, each player should end up with 13 cards, and the last card dealt is to the dealer. It is courtesy to wait for all cards to be dealt before looking at any of your own, and advisable to count your own cards face downwards to check you have 13, before looking at them. If any player does not have 13 cards there has been a misdeal, and there will be less disappointment if no one has seen their cards when a re-deal is necessary.

You may have noted that only three of the players were involved in the deal: West shuffled, East cut, South dealt. North had nothing to do and bridge players hate to waste time. So at rubber bridge you usually find two decks of cards in use, though not on the same deal. These must have different backs to avoid the chaos that would ensue if they were, by error, mixed. North shuffles the second deck ready for the next deal. In this case, having shuffled the deck North places it to his right, by West, who will be the dealer the next time. *(See diagrams on next page.)*

Remember, everything done in turn goes round to the left, including the task of dealing. If South dealt the first deal, West will deal the next, e.g.

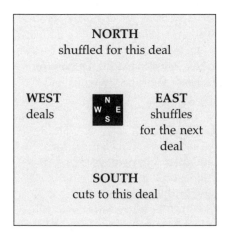

The placing of the deck for the next deal will also remind the players whose turn it is to deal next. A ditty,

> *'If of sense you are bereft,*
> *place the cards upon your left.*
> *If you're not demented quite,*
> *place the cards upon your right'*

aids shufflers to recall where they place the shuffled deck.

Appendix B

Contacts to find your nearest bridge teacher or bridge club:

The English Bridge Union
Broadfields, Bicester Road, Aylesbury HP19 8AZ
☎ 01296 317200   Website: www.ebu.co.uk

The Scottish Bridge Union
56/14 Timber Bush, Edinburgh EH6 6QH
☎ 0131 555 2595   Website: www.sbu.dircon.co.uk

The Welsh Bridge Union
31, Deri Road, Penylan, Cardiff CF23 5AH
☎ 029 2025 5162   Website: www. wbu.org.uk

The Northern Ireland Bridge Union
1, Lenamore Drive, Jordanstown, Belfast BT37 0PQ
☎ 028 9086 2179   Website: www.nibu.co.uk

The Contract Bridge Association of Ireland
Templeogue House, Templeogue Rd, Dublin 6W
☎ +353 (0)1 492 9666   Website: www.cbai.ie

On the Internet:

Bridge News and Links: www.ecatsbridge.com

Viewing: www.bridgebase.com

Bridge Play: www.bridgebase.com
              (free but, being North American-based,
              not many users play Acol)

              www.bridgeclublive.com
              (free trial period, the majority of users plays Acol)